WAKING
UP &
GROWING
UP

WAKING UP & GROWING UP

Spiritual Cross-Training
for an Evolving World

DIANE MUSHO HAMILTON
& GABRIEL KAIGEN WILSON

SHAMBHALA

Shambhala Publications, Inc.
2129 13th Street
Boulder, Colorado 80302
www.shambhala.com

Interior design: Kate Huber-Parker

9 8 7 6 5 4 3 2 1

First Edition
Printed in the United States of America

Shambhala Publications makes every effort
to print on acid-free, recycled paper.
Shambhala Publications is distributed worldwide by
Penguin Random House, Inc., and its subsidiaries.

Library of Congress Cataloging-in-Publication Data
Names: Hamilton, Diane Musho, author. | Wilson, Gabriel Kaigen, author.
Title: Waking up and growing up: spiritual cross-training for an evolving world /
Diane Musho Hamilton and Gabriel Kaigen Wilson.
Description: First edition. | Boulder, Colorado: Shambhala, [2025] |
Includes bibliographical references. |
Identifiers: LCCN 2024034230 | ISBN 9781645473114 (trade paperback)
Subjects: LCSH: Zen Buddhism. | Meditation. | Enlightenment (Buddhism)
Classification: LCC BQ9262.3 .H36 2025 | DDC 294.3/927—dc23/eng/20240904
LC record available at https://lccn.loc.gov/2024034230

The authorized representative in the EU for product safety and
compliance is eucomply OÜ, Pärnu mnt 139b-14, 11317 Tallinn, Estonia,
hello@eucompliancepartner.com.

To Naya

and all the future Buddhas

CONTENTS

INTRODUCTION

Several years before Gabe turned twenty-two, he had a medical crisis that confronted him with his own mortality and thrust him unceremoniously into becoming a spiritual seeker. He began meditating with no real guidance, groping in the dark with questions of ultimate concern, like What is death? What is life, for that matter? Who am I? And what is worth pursuing in the face of death?

These questions had a life of their own. Gabe was gripped by them and felt increasingly alienated from his friend groups who were not provoked by these same questions. For them, getting good grades, making money, founding the next big startup, or becoming famous still held water.

Gabe recalls a loneliness setting in that made him feel small and overwhelmed by the enormity of the world and its contradictions. He felt this most acutely after college when he moved to San Francisco and took frequent rides on the bus through the city. Those bus rides were a highly potent dose of humanity in all its flavors and colors. On a bus trip, you could see a high-powered consultant in a suit and tie, briefcase in hand, standing next to a slumped-over, sleeping body dressed in black garbage bags for underwear and pants. Affluence and abundance sat right next to suffering and poverty while an air of impersonal distance pervaded the whole atmosphere. This juxtaposition was confusing and painful to him.

Only San Francisco could produce such a vast array of identities and embodiments as the bus picked people up along its route from Little Italy to Chinatown, stopping through the financial district and then rolling across into the Castro. On one level, the kaleidoscope of humanity was delightful to him, but at the same time, the diversity created tension in his body and sensations of being separate and cautious. Gabe longed for an experience of togetherness.

Still looking for connection, he eventually bumped into other seekers in chance encounters in a line at Starbucks or during a late-night conversation. These moments were like finding water in the middle of the desert. Finding that he was not alone reenchanted Gabe's life, and he discovered like-minded seekers all around him. It was just a matter, as he recalls, "of looking up and out of my loneliness." It is a marvel at how obvious it is to see and feel others who are awake to this moment.

As Gabe began taking meditation more seriously, he jumped into the world of meditation retreats, meeting practitioners his age who had already devoted years of their lives to a contemplative way of being. There was a calmness, a piercing presence, and a clarity in them that was attractive, even magnetizing, to Gabe. But he also saw that outside of a meditation retreat or spiritual community, these same people did not function well in the world. They relied on a retreat center's controlled and pristine environment to be calm, present, and clear. Maybe the spiritual rigor was real, but it was also a persona these young practitioners hid behind to avoid confronting how the world outside the monastery or retreat life would challenge them to grow.

This prompted Gabe to reflect on what he desired from spiritual practice. He said, "If spiritual training did not empower me to be in the world with skillful means, then it was not for me. I wanted a spirituality with teeth. I wanted clarity and wisdom to be joined with capabilities that made me effective in the world." He was looking for spiritual cross-training and found exactly that in Diane Musho Hamilton, a rigorously trained Soto Zen teacher and a masterful conflict mediator.

Diane founded the Office of Alternative Dispute Resolution in Utah, introducing mediation to the courts. She has mediated everything under the sun and has received numerous peacemaker awards for her work. She often says that "mediate" and "meditate" share the same purpose: to bring what is divided or in dispute into harmony. She has been a meditation practitioner for over forty years, with her journey beginning at Naropa University where she met her root teacher, Chögyam Trungpa Rinpoche. Years later, after raising her son, who has Down syndrome, she committed to the Soto Zen path under the guidance of Genpo Merzel Roshi. From him, she received dharma transmission, and was empowered to teach and pass on the Zen lineage to future generations. She herself is now a *Roshi*, an honorary title given to a Zen teacher.

Following in her footsteps, Gabe also became a facilitator out in the world, helping teams and communities navigate some of the most salient cultural and societal challenges of our times, from race relations to climate change. We also lead transformational seminars for facilitators. Our basic assumption is that the more intimate and aware we can be with ourselves, the more intimate and effective we can be with other people. And, of course, we train rigorously in the Zen context, which this entire book is in service of bringing you into. As of this writing, we have been in a student-teacher relationship for eleven years and counting.

Fast-forward to 2022: On a warm summer night in Boulder, Colorado, during the pandemic, we were with Nikko Odiseos, the president of Shambhala Publications, having just eaten dinner in a makeshift outdoor diner. As we walked downtown back to the Shambhala office, we mused over the benefits of Buddhist practice, the virtues of meditation, and the appeal of Buddhist philosophy. We reflected on the powerful zeitgeist of the 1960s and 1970s that had led to the exploration of consciousness, the human potential movement, and visions for a more wakeful future. The pleasure of recalling that time gave way to Nikko's lament that Buddhist study and practice seem to be waning among the millennial and Z generations. He said that younger people were just not coming to Buddhadharma in the way they had in previous eras.

We flashed on Gabe's experience of being twenty-two years old, seeking, lonely, and lacking a map of what a "spirituality with teeth" looked like. If he had known what to look for, maybe he could have cut through some of the noise and discovered a Buddhist practice (or other tradition) that would satisfy his spiritual seeking and prepare him to be in the world. The next thing we knew, Nikko encouraged us to write a book that provided seekers a map of what spiritual cross-training could look like. And so, we began brainstorming on how to write about our practice to provide questions, perspectives, and guidance to younger generations of seekers.

Waking Up, Growing Up

Gabe had tried out a number of different meditation styles and practice settings, but what it came down to, he says, "was finding a teacher I trusted, respected, and felt I had something to learn from. I had the basic intuition that I could be successful in life by following myself but that a real teacher would take me beyond my notions of who I am and what I could become. I used to joke and say if I could not find that person, I was destined to become a 'millennial desperado.'" Since meeting Diane and joining her practice community, Gabe is like a fish released back into the water.

Some people think Gabe's choice is unusual. Many people now are looking for spiritual scenes that are more fresh, exciting, and accessible. Some want a practice that will take them to the "Next Level," so to speak, while others aspire to become blissful warriors or changemakers for a better world. Others are entrepreneurs or influencers who want to have fun, make money, and give back, as they say, after some serious party time.

The great wisdom traditions seem too old for that, too plodding and serious in their approach to transformation. A lifestyle of sitting still and concentrated study looks completely medieval in a time when we need to build our brand on social media. The great traditions surely don't hold the allure or the rush of the upgrade people are looking for in their contemporary lives.

There is nothing inherently wrong with a good festival. These gatherings can generate renewed energy and opportunities for self-expression and stretching one's perceived limits and boundaries. They can encourage more creativity and exuberance and show us how to enjoy life and genuinely celebrate.

But life isn't a festival. It includes all kinds of difficult challenges from unexpected heartbreak to financial setbacks, dashed expectations, or unexpected losses. We need a spiritual practice that goes beyond feeling good so that we are equipped to respond when pain inevitably arises or things go badly. In the Zen tradition, the method is to learn how to sit still for an hour, for a day, for seven days, to discover who and what we really are. We refer to this path as the *Wholehearted Way*, an approach that includes our entire life and its myriad challenges. The open-heartedness we discover through sitting is fulfilling, dependable, and not exclusive to getting what we want.

This book encourages our readers to invest in a spiritual practice that will sustain them through life's ups and downs. As we considered this question together, we asked some people in our community at Two Arrows Zen in Salt Lake City their views. We asked them to describe some of the challenges that bring them to the practice and why they think Zen training is suited for our times. We wondered aloud what brings them to the zendo, why they return, and how sitting with a community satisfies their longing for meaning and purpose.

Everyone seemed eager to engage these questions and agreed on certain things. They acknowledged that we live in rapidly changing times when unique and pressing concerns like climate change, economic disparity, and the exponential expansion of technology are creating anxiety and stress in people. Buddha taught that life is suffering, but somehow the scale and unfamiliarity of these threats can feel more overwhelming than one's personal confrontation with sickness, old age, and death.

They spoke about the tremendous overload of online information and the difficulty assessing what is true. There are so many opinions with entire online cultures built to support them. It is as though the algorithms inform our beliefs and worldviews rather than philosophy, religious training, education, or civic engagement. They expressed concern that using our tech devices with quick internet and social media access has contributed to an inability to focus very long. They feel prone to distractions, and someone even suggested that sitting still might be more difficult for us than earlier generations.

They also spoke about the significant emphasis put on identity in many of the contexts in which they live and work. There seems to be sustained pressure to identify with subgroups related to race, ethnicity, gender, sexual orientation, and political causes in the effort to secure social justice. While they supported the collective efforts toward fairness and equity, the heightening of difference in many contexts excludes deepening the shared values that create unity and coherence at work and in our communities. They talked about the stress of picking up so many identities rather than putting them down.

We aim to share the wisdom and support that a 2,500-year-old spiritual path offers. Zen practice challenges our conventional mind, acquisitive tendencies, and fixation on achievement. It doesn't promise the "Next Level" experience. Rather, it offers steady presence, open-heartedness, and a time-honored lineage and community. This practice addresses our deepest existential longing and has stood the test of time. Zen practice reduces stress, builds resilience, and nurtures compassion in life's challenging moments.

The great spiritual traditions continue to have the rich, unique, and unparalleled ability to speak to our human potential. Through generations, the traditions have refined their body of teachings and honed their practices to explore the depths of being human, instructing us to express care for each other and our world. They encourage us to clarify our purpose, and they provide us with direction in life. And because they encourage us to connect with something greater than ourselves, they provide a profound sense of meaning and fulfillment.

Our tradition is Soto Zen, and we hope to convey to you the wonders of sitting meditation, dharma study, and the student-teacher relationship, and how these are powerful vehicles for recognizing our universal unconditioned nature and cultivating a set of perennial human values. In our practice, we refer to opening to our universal nature as "Waking Up."[1]

But spiritual practitioners need everyday skill sets and so do our organizations. Leadership, governance, fundraising, and effective administration are essential to our success. We need communication training and conflict resolution. These skills are referred to as "Growing Up." Diane watched while several of her spiritual communities collapsed during times of stress because the groups didn't have the life skills to go through the challenges differently. Many contemporary spiritual communities implode when faced with stress, crisis, or scandal because these skills are lacking. People imagine the conflicts should never have arisen in the first place or naively expect humanness to evaporate into bliss and oneness. When this doesn't happen, communities fall apart.

Gabe also finds that among his generation, spiritual communities can be places young practitioners go to hide out and, frankly, not address the healing, skill building, and development they need in order to serve others. What good is waking up to our universal nature if we can't enact this insight because our emotional and interpersonal skills remain undeveloped or we have yet to learn how to use our power and vitality to serve the whole rather than hurt and divide?

We must embody our insight and manifest the teaching in our lives and in our communities. This book refers to practices that reveal our universal nature and bring forth energies like love, compassion, and forgiveness as the domain of Waking Up. Additionally, it includes practices that mature our interpersonal and emotional skills in the process of Growing Up. The first five chapters of the book explore the theme of Growing Up. While chapters 6 through 16 delve into the theme of Waking Up.

Spiritual Cross-Training

The distinctions of *waking up* and *growing up* come from Ken Wilber, an American writer and philosopher with a unique genius for pattern recognition that he applied to the field of human development. Wilber has pioneered thinking on how spiritual traditions can and should include Western psychological work, emotional development, and relationship skills as part of spiritual practice. His integral theory asserts that nurturing a healthy ego with positive psychology is compatible with Zen's letting go of the ego because each method works on different dimensions of our being. His view is that they are highly complementary; hence the word *spiritual cross-training*.

This book brings you inside our integrally informed Zen practice that deliberately trains in Waking Up and Growing Up. While it draws on the timeless teachings of the Zen masters, it also weaves insights from neurophysiology, trauma work, adult development, shadow processes, emotional maturity, and conflict resolution skills. Although human development is time bound and contingent, a developmental framework helps us clarify what it means for adults to continue to thrive, nourishing their communities, places of work, and families.

Buddhism in the West is a fledgling enterprise. In order to be attractive to a younger generation and relevant to our times, it needs to deepen and grow sustainably, and the lineages must evolve. They must meet traditional needs and expectations but include modern scientific insights and postmodern cultural skills. The lineages should change as human culture changes, and when insights arise from psychology, evolutionary biology, neuroscience, and ecology, they should be integrated into our spiritual practice.[2]

Recognizing our deepest nature supports personal and collective growth, so we may become mature and wholehearted in our social interactions. This is the approach we take in our practice, and it serves our work as mediators and group facilitators. We assume it will help our readers with their work in the world.

All spiritual endeavors emphasize cultivating qualities such as loving-kindness, compassion, generosity, and empathy toward others. These traits contribute to stronger relationships and greater connection to our communities and the world. Rather than canceling and exiling each other, our differences can be worked with, and our shared commitments can strengthen relationships. Deeper self-awareness should translate into more durable relationships, but it doesn't happen without practice.

Drawing on our experience, we hope to inspire and build confidence in you about the value of spiritual cross-training. We will offer examples of working with one's ego while deepening the recognition of the awakened state, of ethical training, relationship work, and practicing in a feedback-rich environment with others. With this integrated approach, we equip practitioners to navigate the crises of our time with presence, wisdom, and compassion. Spiritual cross-training empowers us to confront adversity while nurturing a positive future, echoing the teachings of Shakyamuni Buddha on the path to liberation. We hope that your greatest aspirations for awakening and growth are supported through this work.

May your practice be of benefit to others.

WAKING
UP &
GROWING
UP

ZEN AND GROWING UP

Diane Musho Hamilton

Evolution is the way in which the person is settling the issue
of what is self and what is other. —Robert Kegan

Zen is the consummate "Waking Up" school. Its singular purpose,
through the practice of sitting meditation, is to offer a direct experience of our deepest nature and our interconnectedness with all
things. Waking up involves a profound shift from identification with
our self-image, personal concerns, preferences, and stories. Through
sitting upright with focused attention and open awareness, our very
identity shifts from I, me, and mine to that which is greater than me.
This shift leads to a deep sense of liberation, clarity, and compassion.

I have been a seeker for most of my life and began to meditate
when I was in my early twenties. The notion of awakening or enlightenment was very familiar to me by the time I was introduced to the
work of Ken Wilber in my early forties. But Ken made an important
distinction that has influenced the way that I practice and teach in the
Buddhist tradition. He introduced the idea of "Growing Up" into the
domain of spiritual practice. Growing up refers to adult development,
and emphasizes how adults, like children, continue to mature, learn,
and develop throughout their lives.

Wilber has mapped many different theorists along different lines of development. He notes their models can range from four levels to eight, twelve, sixteen, or more. This growth trajectory is built into our evolution and occurs sequentially, with one stage unfolding into the next. Over the course of a lifetime, if the conditions are right, the perspective of human beings expands, their skills become more nuanced and complex, and their artistry grows.[1] Just as plants flourish in the right light, temperature, and humidity, humans will thrive or struggle to develop, depending on their circumstances.

While waking up opens us to the boundless, timeless dimension of existence, growing up tracks the evolution of our worldviews, relationship skills, ethical choices, and aesthetic concerns. Growing up accrues over time as we develop new insights and skills, while waking up is not concerned with achievement or acquisition of any kind. It is the recognition of our inherent wholeness and innate well-being—unconditioned and ever present.

Here is an example that illustrates this idea. When I was a new Zen teacher, I remember a young man who came to a retreat, or *sesshin*, I was leading in Southern Utah. A Zen sesshin is rigorous, beginning zazen at 6:00 a.m. On the first morning, the young man failed to come to sit. Our custom is to have a conversation when anyone misses morning zazen and remind them of the protocols. I happened to walk by this man's tent after breakfast, and he was standing outside, so I walked over to check in with him about the sitting schedule.

I expected a straightforward conversation but instead was met by rebellious, even aggressive energy. He was a big man with a bold demeanor—think Andrew Tate at a meditation retreat. Rather than simply hearing me out, he asserted that he wasn't doing what everyone else was doing. He said he would participate in the retreat in his own way according to his preferences. I asked him about his intention in coming to the retreat. He replied again with a deluge of "I, me, and mine" statements infused with willfulness and bravado. I told him that while I respected his autonomy, this retreat was a group practice involving full participation with the schedule and community. He said that didn't interest him, so I said, "Well, then, it is probably best for you to go."

I walked away feeling a little sad that I had asked him to leave, but I didn't feel angry or disappointed. I felt disrespected, for sure, but I also recognized that he saw the world through an egocentric lens—the viewpoint exclusive to one's self-interest. From a developmental perspective, he was right where he needed to be. But he didn't belong in a Zen sesshin because in our practice, sitting and working together is paramount. We will explore waking up later in the book, but let's see first how our identity grows and changes in developmental stages.

Imperial Identity

The imperial identity is a very early stage of human development. It is referred to as "egocentric" by Ken Wilber and "imperial" in the work of Robert Kegan, a psychologist who taught and conducted his research at Harvard. The imperial identity experiences security when it has control over its environment. It prefers social settings where relationships are unrestricted or not bound by conformist conventions. The imperial personality needs freedom to satisfy its immediate needs. A traditional Zen retreat offends the imperial identity by emphasizing group norms like structured practice, the enforcement of silence, and timeliness. Zen practice is a highly socialized space against which our imperial drives stand out in sharp contrast. It provides an excellent context to study our imperial, often impulsive, selves.

Autonomy, security, and immediate gratification are central to the imperial identity. Zen practice makes these drives objects of attention so that we can begin to consciously work with them instead of being dominated by them. For example, the request to be seated in the zendo five minutes before the start of the sitting period gives us an opportunity to observe how well we can relinquish our preferences to simply adhere to the schedule. Two to three days into a retreat, people will begin to show up at the very last second, dashing into the zendo before the doors close. This pattern expresses a stressful negotiation between the imperial and socialized dimensions of self, which most of us will recognize in ourselves.

Sitting meditation is challenging to the imperial identity. Individual wants, needs, and preferences arise while we are meditating. Instead of indulging in the instant gratification of adjusting our posture, scratching our nose, or getting up to take a bio break, we simply observe the distractions and then let them go until the bell sounds. This ability to defer and adapt, focusing on sitting still, is a developmental achievement of the next wave of adult maturity, the socialized self.

The Zen container creates powerful group coherence, which carries the practice for everyone. Yet, some of us continue to assert autonomy, as if to ensure we don't lose it. However, healthy development involves transcending earlier stages while including the energy and achievements of each prior wave. Healthy autonomy remains even as we adhere to social norms. So, we can participate fully in the group, and when it comes time to party at the end of the retreat, the imperial self returns, happy to throw back shots of whiskey, enjoy beats, and dance late into the night.

Usually, but not always, most people complete the egocentric stage in childhood or adolescence. The all-important next stage is referred to as "ethnocentric" by Wilber or the "socialized self," according to Kegan. This next stage of development occurs as humans learn to subjugate their preferences to the purpose and well-being of the group to which they belong, whether it is their family, tribe, religious group, military unit, or sports team. This stage usually marks the beginning of the adult stages.

Socialized Identity

All great religious traditions are built on the developmental achievements of what Kegan refers to as the socialized self. Religious groups promote the values of belonging, obedience, duty, self-sacrifice, and loyalty, which are probably why the traditions have survived for so long. Social obligations underpin these values, whether concerning the family or the religious tradition. At their best, relationships are further cultivated through generosity, compassion, forgiveness, and altruism.

From a traditional worldview, family and belonging are considered essential to human well-being. This is true across cultures. The specifics vary, but within any traditional culture, there is a powerful sense of the group's boundaries, and according to behavioral codes, you are inside of those boundaries or you are not. There are no shades of gray for the traditionalist. You are either in or you are out. Security derives from conformity to the group and its beliefs. Punishment or exile for violating group boundaries occurs in traditional contexts. In contrast, differences from other groups are feared, even maligned, and an "us vs. them" mentality reinforces the group's codes and rules, keeping members in line. Most communication reifies group values, and dissent isn't permitted in this wave of development, even in conversation.

From the perspective of an individual, the socialized self represents a powerful developmental leap from egocentrism, characterized by a new capacity to conform. Where the imperial voice would say, "I am my wants, needs, and desires," the socialized identity values the group's wants, needs, and desires above its own. It accepts the group's thoughts, beliefs, and moral codes in order to belong. Socialized identities turn to external sources of authority for direction and validation of their sense of self, avoiding any confrontation with this authority.

The community is central to the traditional or socialized self. Rituals like graduations, weddings, and funerals reinforce belonging, deepen bonds, and contribute to predictability in life. Attendance at these events displays loyalty, care, and commitment. Familiarity is paramount, and safety is an all-important dimension of culture, and a reliable community provides it. These qualities are deeply embedded in religious traditions, serving humanity over generations by creating stability, order, cultural coherence, ethical conduct, and meaning.

It is also true that many people have left the religion of their upbringing precisely because of the prevalence of "us vs. them," the inability to question and think freely, the critical judgments of other groups, and the pressure to conform to all the social norms. The ethical breaches among community members, and the hypocrisy, also become intolerable for some people. But as we develop and change, it is easy to take for granted the tremendous cohesion that emerged with this wave of human endeavor.

Traditional conventions remain in Zen practice but generally are not understood through a developmental lens. For example, when people come to explore Zen in most contexts, the highly socialized structures are not explained. Newcomers are simply expected to participate in the formal conventions, strict time frames, obeisance to authority, et cetera, without being able to ask questions such as, Why are the Zen forms and routines so exact? Why does the tradition still rely on such a strict hierarchy of priests and teachers? Why are talks given in a way that ignores questioning and other adult learning principles? How is power distributed throughout the community?

The simple answer to these questions is that these conventions are vestiges of Zen traditionalism. The emphasis on structure, schedule, rules of conduct, and hierarchy all serve to create tremendous order and stability. The discipline it takes to enact these conventions strengthens character and deepens resolve. This training is "old school," so to speak. That is not to say that "old school" doesn't have its downsides, but for building a sound practice and an enduring lineage, these attributes still provide an unshakable foundation.

I didn't grow up with a particularly strong religious education. My family was Latter-day Saints, but we were called Jack Mormons. This phrase is used to indicate cultural, non-church-going Mormons, and it captures my family's sensibility. We had a very relaxed relationship with our church and our creator. As children, our ethical training came from our mother and father's good sense and modeling. We were never urged to conform socially or told what to believe. Nor were my parents inclined to use an "us and them" framework, except when devout relatives felt the urge to proselytize. And then my mother rolled her eyes while my father ignored them.

So, it struck my parents as strange when I veered toward studying and practicing Eastern spirituality. They really couldn't make sense of sitting meditation or silent retreats. When I shaved my head to ordain in the Zen lineage, my father asked me whether, like Britney Spears, it was a cry for help. He was kidding, but he was serious. Although they didn't understand my involvement with the practice, my mother and father were never intolerant of my choice. I believe they appreciated its influence on me. As a student of Ram Dass once said of his mother, "She doesn't like my Buddhism, but she loves it when I'm the Buddha."

Like me, many people approach Zen with very little in the way of religious training. Some people who arrive to explore the practice are spiritual-but-not-religious types. Others are science or business types looking for stress reduction. Buddhism appeals to a secular worldview because it doesn't require petitionary prayer or a belief in a deity. Many others have come from a background in a religious tradition like Christianity, Islam, or Judaism but have moved on for various reasons. But they carry an embodied memory of similar traditional forms.

Some people are allergic to the formalities and rituals, so these elements present an obstacle to group practice. Others seem very at home with these aspects of tradition: discipline is familiar, group belonging comes easily, and they enjoy the synchronization of rituals and their positive impact on their nervous systems. But if they are from the West and are interested in Zen, they have, most likely, evolved from a singularly socialized worldview to the next powerful stage of development.

Self-Authoring Identity

When people differentiate from a socialized worldview, they move to a stage called "world-centric" by Ken Wilber or "self-authoring" by Robert Kegan. *Worldcentric* describes someone who has moved beyond exclusive identity with their group and identifies much more broadly with humanity. This points to a sense of self that is flexible, curious, and open to cultural differences rather than being afraid of them.

This worldview has the capacity to include more. It values diversity, inclusion, travel, and education, engaging many different perspectives. People whose center of gravity is worldcentric usually appreciate the different flavors of the great traditions. Environmental principles and care for the earth come powerfully online at this developmental phase. Science is valued, and social and economic justice is a genuine concern for the worldcentric self.

Kegan's language of self-authoring also describes a developmental leap on the personal level. The person transitioning from the traditional, socialized stage to the self-authoring stage sometimes feels they have been released from jail. They are freed from a sense of self that is embedded in social relationships with their long list of obligations. They can now choose to go skiing on Christmas rather than attending church services, even though their relatives might disapprove.

Unlike the raw rebelliousness of the imperial stage, the choice of the self-authoring individual is not rejecting socialized norms but simply moving toward their individual fulfillment. They can enact or let go of the strict prescriptions for how to live, depending instead on their internalized values and ethical codes for direction. They are free to ask themselves questions about what they personally want or need in life. At the same time, at this stage, one can make decisions in favor of group norms because they choose to, not because they are compelled to.

Robert Kegan says that at this stage of development, a self emerges that is stable across different social spheres and settings.[2] This means the individual is less dependent on the group for identity and can move more fluidly between circumstances and cultures. Unlike the traditional self, one is no longer embedded in relationships but can now *have* them. The feelings of guilt, shame, or anxiety that would formerly keep the traditional person conforming to group norms are successfully overcome. Decisions are made in service of autonomy and one's personal authority without the need for the immediate gratification of the egocentric stage.

Many of the students I have worked with over the years in the Zen context reflect this worldview. The practice supports the developmental task of exploring the self, becoming more deeply authentic, and discerning what is most meaningful in life. There is a much greater sense of individuality and autonomy than you will find in students in the socialized wave of development. There seems to be an ability to take responsibility for one's choices, reveal one's personal pain, disclose doubts and vulnerabilities, and engage in reciprocity with the community. Kegan says at this stage, "Reciprocity now becomes a matter of mutually preserving one another's distinctness while interdependently fashioning a bigger context in which these separate identities can function."[3]

One wonders how these evolving worldviews relate to the Buddha's doctrine of no self, particularly at the stage of development when self-orientation predominates again in the developmental journey. Wilber says that insight into the Buddha's realization of no permanent, unchanging self or essence can happen at any level of development.[4] But as identity becomes less fixed, this insight is more accessible and easily stabilized.

But for some practitioners, the exploration of self-identity is far more compelling than the emptiness of self-identity. I worked with a student for about ten years who showed up at the zendo highly committed to practice. Still, between intensive practice periods, she spent her free time exploring different healing modalities and consciousness work until she finally settled on guiding psychedelic experiences. I didn't see a conflict between her Zen practice and her psychedelic work, but she did. She was fascinated by the content of the psyche rather than the open, boundless, and unconditioned space of mind, so she moved on. I would have liked to see her complete her training, but I'm confident that her years of Zen practice inform the work that she does now.

In the world of lay practice, one can observe the difference between the egocentric, Andrew Tate–type practitioner and the self-authoring practitioner, whose ego is far less demanding and fixed. However, for some, conflicts between the exploration of their authenticity and the demands of Zen practice cannot be resolved. Some people find it too difficult to give up other personal interests to deepen their sitting practice. The demands of lay life, including children, work, and even time for rest or a vacation, interfere with a sustained, regular practice. The hierarchy of the student-teacher relationship can be problematic for self-authoring types. Although they might desire contact with a teacher, they are simply not willing to confer spiritual authority to someone else when they are in a phase of becoming self-responsible and sovereign. They aren't available to challenge their self-identity or to disrupt their habitual patterns, which is completely fair. The flavor of this kind of practice is an acquired taste.

But for those students who can resolve these conflicts, or at least keep the contradictions in play, the practice gives them a genuine spiritual orientation, a set of instructions in the form of teachings, a coherent practice community, and a method for responding to their deepest questions. Meditation supports growth from one stage of development to the next, and many years of meditation practice can lead to a "kosmic-centric worldview"[5] or what Kegan calls the "self-transforming mind."

Self-Transforming Identity

Eventually, one will emerge from the preoccupation with one's own authenticity, autonomy, and self-regulation. We discover freedom from the grip of self-orientation. It becomes easier and easier to relax without constant internal references to I, me, and mine, and to reside as awareness itself. Attention is open and available from moment to moment without the compulsively grasping onto beliefs, relationships, or curated experiences of the self-authoring stage. At the self-authoring stage, our very life is a project, and there can be relief in relaxing our attachment to another great experience.

According to Robert Kegan's research, about 1 percent of the population falls into the self-transforming category. Most importantly, this stage of adult development is characterized by an interest in the transformation of one's own identity and beliefs. What emerges is the capacity to simultaneously entertain multiple perspectives and engage in complex thinking without stress. The ability to "take a perspective on our perspective" allows for other points of view to inform and shape our understanding.

We find that our persistent need to know, draw firm conclusions, and defend our position in conversation is vastly reduced. We recognize that while some things are known, much remains unknown, and even more is unknowable. Our attempts to grasp and retain knowledge relax, even as our pleasure in learning is heightened. Kegan says that this self-transforming stage of development involves humility and openness to learning and growth, and we become increasingly willing to revise our beliefs and integrate new information.[6]

These traits are very apparent in conversation. I am reminded of a discussion I had with two colleagues about our views on the relevance of shadow work to spiritual practice. I remember one of my companions was very passionate about his views to the point of being strident, insistent, and dominating. I became argumentative as I resisted his overbearing opinions. The contrast with my other colleague was striking. He seemed to enjoy every aspect of the conversation, even smiling during the struggles. He didn't become anxious, nor did he withdraw. He was consistently present and interested, asking far more questions than people usually do, offering his own perspectives, and doing an excellent job of listening. There was immense freedom in his participation. I will never forget that contrast. It made the conversation so generative, rich, and enjoyable. He will forever be a model in my mind of how to engage multiple perspectives.

Zen practice encourages not-knowing, or beginner's mind, in which one approaches each moment with openness and curiosity.

It promotes a deep exploration of the nature of the self, constant change, and the interconnectedness of all things. Its emphasis on objectless, open awareness undermines our clinging to fixed concepts of self. With practice, one functions freely with or without identity, and nonattachment is a living reality. Serving others is the expression of an authentic Zen practice, and generous activity and concern for others is natural and easy without the relentless preoccupation with self.

Ken Wilber assigns the label of kosmic-centric consciousness to this stage of development, which includes a greater ability to be cognitively flexible and emotionally mature. It describes expanding beyond personal identity to a universal perspective that includes all things. Even the worldcentric, ethnocentric, and egocentric perspectives may arise, inform, and easily disappear. As we said earlier, healthy development means that we can include earlier worldviews without being captured by them. In other words, we can both transcend and include previous perspectives.

At this stage, we recognize the interconnectedness and interdependence of all things, and there is a natural, enduring appreciation for the vastness, complexity, and diversity of the kosmos. Zen Master Dogen Zenji's famous line that we "study the self to forget the self"[7] is echoed in Ken Wilber's description of kosmic-centered consciousness. According to him, our perception shifts to the inherent unity of all things and the suffering of all beings. We are moved to compassionate action, with the view that everything is ours to care for. Our capacity for love and compassion is much greater as we widen to embrace those who, at earlier stages, would have been "othered."

The kosmic-centric self points to far less preoccupation with our personal, limited life. Our sense of space and time changes. We can experience the precision and particularity of this immediate moment, but we see the domain beyond time, so we no longer practice Zen to attain. Instead, we sit because that is what Buddhas do. The student-teacher duality dissolves. The forms are fine with us, and so is the schedule. We like to practice with others and are happy to be alone. We become sincerely available to the immediacy of every precious day of practice and the joy that comes from ordinary activity, and we are able to face death when the time comes. That our practice is our whole life is the greatest spiritual achievement in the Zen school, and when this insight occurs, it is clear that waking up and growing up are one and the same thing.

2

EMBODIED SKILLS FOR RELATIONSHIPS

Gabriel Kaigen Wilson

> To change, people must become aware of their sensations
> and how their bodies interact with the world around them.
> —Bessel A. van der Kolk

Once, I was co-facilitating a diversity workshop, and my colleague stood outside the door, greeting participants as they came in. He was offering the standards: "Hello," "Welcome," and "How are you?" But as I tuned in more, I sensed that his greetings were warmer toward some and cooler toward other participants. His interaction with any one participant was no more than a couple of seconds, but with some, his handshake was a little longer, his smile slightly brighter, and his tone of voice deeper and more animated. He was warmer to the people of color than to the White participants. The different impacts on participants were interesting to watch and feel. Those who received the warmth seemed like they had felt a refreshing breeze on a warm day. But those who were recipients of his coolness subtly pulled inward, head tucked and eyes cast down, like when a wind gust picks up. For the entirety of that workshop, I stayed focused on the nonverbal dimensions of everyone's interactions.

At one point, we engaged in a paired activity to practice active listening. I scanned over the room and eventually settled my attention on one pair of participants. The speaker seemed like they were enjoying their communication. Their face was expressive and their gestures animated. The listener was relaxed, attentive, and interested. Then, the speaker clearly said something that bothered the listener, who then crossed their arms and leaned back to continue "listening." The speaker became less animated in their gestures and facial expressions, and their speech pattern shifted from fluid to truncated, tripping over their words.

At the end of that workshop, I remember wondering to myself, How much of our interpersonal interactions are empowered or constrained by the nonverbal impact we have on one another? In fact, there is a term for this: *neuroception*, the subconscious perception of safety or threat cues by our autonomic nervous system. Some dimension of ourselves is subtly attuned to the nonverbal layer of our interactions—such as facial expressions, vocal tone, and body language—scanning for whether we are safe in a relationship or whether the other person threatens our perspective, values, or well-being.

This term was coined by Dr. Stephen Porges, a distinguished neuroscientist and professor of psychiatry, best known for developing what is known as polyvagal theory.[1] The theory provides a neurobiological framework that explores the nervous system's role in regulating social interactions, emotional experiences, and responses to stress. Central to this theory is the description of the ventral vagus nerve, a nerve in mammals that runs from the brain through the neck to the heart and abdomen and helps regulate the facial and head muscles. This nerve coordinates changes in our heart rate with movements in our facial muscles. In this way, our hearts are literally projected through our faces for others to see and feel.

According to Porges, we should pay attention to three major state shifts in the autonomic nervous system. The first is "rest and digest," in which the system is relaxed, senses safety, and makes positive social contact. Next is the "fight-or-flight" state, which readies us for quick responsiveness, defense, or mobilization. Finally, "freeze" is the body's most basic attempt to survive by becoming completely immobilized.[2]

Because of our work with interpersonal skill development and conflict resolution, we highly support Porges's emphasis on the nervous system and its relationship to social engagement. In our practice, we pay special attention to how our nervous system affects our social interactions, particularly in the context of difficult conversations and stressful disputes. We explore social connections in regulating or dysregulating our nervous system because, within any dialogue, our bodies are involved in a powerful, immediate, and contagious feeling conversation below the level of speech and the use of language. Because our human nervous systems have evolved to be highly intimate with the nervous systems of the other human beings around us, it is important to learn to co-regulate our nervous systems from moment to moment.

In the social dimension of our Zen practice, when we share the details of our day, describe our emotional ups and downs, engage in abstract ideas, or simply share the dharma, we watch how the ancient defense system constantly looks for safety or threats. We practice familiarizing ourselves with the state of our bodies. We study what the resting state feels like and how easy it is to make contact with others, to sense good faith, and to find agreement. We also look carefully at what dysregulation feels like in the nervous system, how stimulating adrenaline is in the bloodstream, how cognition and memory become impaired, and how social contact is strained. Most importantly, we observe how difference quickly escalates to threat, shifting the entire nervous system from rest and digest to fight-or-flight. Then we practice working with our bodies in real time, using different techniques to calm the body, regulate the nervous system, and restore equilibrium to the mind.

As we learn to pay attention to our bodies and these reactions, we become much more adept at cultivating our social connections, taking into account the state of our bodies. This practice impacts our ability to have successful conversations about challenging topics and deepen our relationships through the exploration of our differences. These skills contribute to resilient, healthy relationships because we develop confidence in navigating difficulty even as we deepen our bonds. Combining mindfulness and an understanding of neurobiology is the cutting edge of our conflict work.

Sameness and Difference

Humans naturally seek safety and avoid danger. Of course, there are always the risk-takers and self-destructive types among us, but collectively, our bodies relax in an atmosphere of safety and move to defend ourselves in the face of danger. In our context of practice, safety equates to commonality, sameness, or agreement in conversation. On the other hand, differences are exciting to the nervous system. Differences disrupt our expectations, startling us into paying attention. They capture our focus and create learning opportunities, but they quickly become perceived as threats. When this happens, the sympathetic nervous system takes over from the parasympathetic nervous system and doses us with adrenaline.

Under adrenaline's influence, all bodily functions change when we become defensive. We stop being able to communicate openly, let alone learn. This defensive response intensifies as the stakes get higher, and differences in opinion become disagreements in our values or belief systems. These disagreements naturally lead to competing strategies for dealing with our issues. In the process, we move from being allies to being adversaries. This is the greatest of our human challenges because our inability to work together to solve problems lies behind every existential threat we face.

So, understanding these embodied states is crucial to our wellbeing. We are most happy, free, and productive in the rest and digest state. We feel safe and make social contact easily. We affirm one another, ascribe good faith, and deepen our bonds. We stabilize our social contact by exchanging safety cues, with kind, supportive facial expressions.

We have the ability to downshift the fight-or-flight response through the use of mental reminders, breath, and social support.

When we sense an atmosphere of safety, sameness, or affiliation, we relax, join with others, make jokes, expose our vulnerabilities, take risks, and generate new ideas. An agreement will register in our nervous system as a safety cue. A genuine smile does the same thing. So does laughter. Cooperative tones of voice, nodding, and uttering "uh-huh's" in conversation all communicate safety. We are creatures who seek out the sensation of sameness and, therefore, safety: in our faces, speech, dress, and, unfortunately, our skin color.

However, the autonomic nervous system is binary, and differences are exciting to it. They register when someone disagrees with us or challenges our position. Facial expressions and tones of voice change, and safety cues disappear. When tensions rise, the autonomic nervous system senses a potential threat, and the sympathetic side takes over. The amygdala sends an alert signal to the nerves of the sympathetic nervous system and to the adrenals. They respond by secreting adrenaline into the bloodstream. The adrenaline causes the heart to beat faster, the pulse to increase, and the blood pressure to go up, preparing us for action.

We breathe more rapidly, taking in oxygen, which increases alertness and sharpens our senses. This happens even in ordinary conversation and affects our ability to work effectively together. Our communications become tense and agitated, and our ability to make positive social contact decreases. Without being aware of it, we often seek ways to defend ourselves or opportunities to withdraw from conversations or problem-solving. Remember that we can lower the stress response and recalibrate to the resting state in social situations, but it takes practice and skill.

Skills for Creating Sameness

The deeper or more reliable our connection to sameness and safety, the more powerfully we can address our differences and learn from them. In human relations, key techniques can be employed to create sameness and to address our differences more successfully. The skills of sameness bridge our minds, hearts, and nervous systems to those of others.

There are many different embodied methods for regulating one's own nervous system when the fight-or-flight response has been triggered. Here are some that we use in our practice. This skill set can be used by individuals or implemented by groups when co-regulation may be helpful in a group setting. Because so much of our work takes place in a group context, practicing embodied regulation techniques is an essential feature of our work.

Cognitive Cues

Because stress hormones in the body create the sensation that something is wrong, it is important to begin with a simple mental reminder that "Everything is okay." Or "I can tolerate these feelings," or "Nothing here is dangerous," or "I can remain present." Everyone chooses their own cognitive cue that gives them the confidence to work with the triggering sensations in their body and learn how to stay present and calm themselves.

Rhythmic Breathing

Engaging the breath is an age-old technique for managing stress in the body. We focus on breath that is rhythmic, meaning that the intervals of the in-breath to the out-breath remain the same. We also advise to lengthen the exhale. So, if the inhale is four beats, then the exhale is six beats. This rhythm is repeated until one senses calm. Remember that according to polyvagal theory, this kind of breathing activates the vagus nerve, eliciting a relaxation response.

Connecting with the Body and Gravity

We find it helpful to ground ourselves by focusing on the body and the points where it interacts with gravity. The instruction is to feel the density of your form, continuing to breathe. Then notice the presence of gravity on your sit bones, legs, feet, and any other place where you can feel its dynamic tension. When fully present with the body, the mind is less likely to be preoccupied with defensive thoughts.

Accessing Space

For meditation practitioners, accessing the sensation of space can be extremely helpful when regulating the stress response. Practice feeling space above, below, and around you. Then extend the sensation through your body and mind so that space is all-pervasive. This is important because stress hormones are designed to bring the body to action. This mobilization can feel intense and, at times, claustrophobic. Reflecting on space literally creates more space in the mind and relaxation in the body.

Social Support

Supportive social contact is extremely effective in helping us to co-regulate our nervous systems. We often practice making gentle eye contact, breathing together for several minutes, or interrupting a challenging conversation to ask the group to feel for a moment or two. Sometimes, we take a straw poll to assess who feels triggered so that people know it is a shared experience and no one is isolated in their anxiety. Then we take a poll to assess when the group has returned to the resting state.

We are such sensitive social creatures that we should strive to include shared methods of co-regulation to lend support and increase the experience of safety in a group. The psychologist Shelley Taylor has suggested the language of "tend and befriend" to indicate acts of caregiving and social support that allow the parasympathetic nervous system to return the body to a state of rest and digest.

Reflective Listening

From a communications perspective, listening is the most powerful tool for restoring equilibrium to the nervous system in a group. Reflective listening creates the experience of sameness, safety, and calm. Once someone joins fully with the experience of another, all division dissolves, and sameness results. This is experienced as safety in the body, showing how our systems are designed to co-regulate.

To truly listen, we pay attention to this moment, hearing what the speaker says, including how they feel and even what they may not be saying. Most importantly, listening involves letting go of the preoccupations of the self, suspending our internal thoughts, and quieting the viewpoints most closely held as "mine."

As easy as that sounds, it takes practice because those silent opinions give us a reference point to hold on to and secure our sense of self. It is like having an internal handrail in the mind. I may behave as though I am listening, but I am deriving a sense of solidity, of safety, of security inside myself. We all know the experience of half listening to someone because we are fixated on our internal viewpoint or opinion.

When we truly listen, we join fully with the speaker's experience—in other words, we become the same as them. The final gesture of listening is to reflect back what the other person has said. These reflections are not merely about ensuring we have captured the content correctly. The test for success is not whether we believe we have listened fully but whether the speaker feels they have been heard.

Asking Questions

Another skill for creating sameness is asking questions. Of course, questions can be posed in the spirit of difference, like in a cross-examination in a courtroom setting. But when they are sincere, questions are the gateway into another's experience. They may convey curiosity and empathy and lead to mutual understanding. It is helpful to distinguish three basic types of questions: open, narrowing, and closed questions.

Open-ended questions are the most inviting because the speaker is free to explore. They work like open invitations—for example, "Why are you here today?" "Tell me about your background." "What is important to you right now?" These questions give the speaker an opportunity to explore and the listener a chance to hear their concerns.

Narrowing questions help deepen and clarify thoughts and feelings. For example, during a five-day facilitation training, Diane taught a sameness module. There was a group of seven or eight participants of Asian descent. With their permission, Diane facilitated a conversation among them as a demonstration called a fishbowl. The intention was to explore how their cultural upbringing shaped their experience, particularly the expression of emotion. The cultures represented in the group were Chinese, Japanese, Taiwanese, and Malaysian.

It was a moving dialogue as they explored their common themes such as picking up unspoken emotional cues, demonstrating respect for elders, and metabolizing shame. There was a moment in the dialogue when Diane noticed something and asked a narrow question to explore. "I'm observing that when you speak, everyone looks at you, but you don't return eye contact when you are the speaker. Do you notice this? Can you help me understand this?"

All the participants in the fishbowl nodded their heads in acknowledgment. They delved into personal reflections that, while different, converged on a theme that Diane drew out. They agreed that they were powerfully conditioned to privilege the social context over their personal experience and to orient their sense of self to others. So, the lack of eye contact was an effort to minimize focus on themselves. This specific question brought the conversation directly into the present and brought everyone else in the room closer to the experience of those in the fishbowl.

Closed questions have only two possible responses: yes or no. "Are you willing to share that story with me?" "Is now a good time to talk about that issue?" Closed-ended questions support open conversation and can establish boundaries or limits. I was recently working with a leadership team. We spent an entire day unpacking certain communication breakdowns, hoping that we could draw lessons and forge a path forward in the team. After unpacking three breakdowns, one of the executive team members was perceptibly moved. I asked her if she would be willing to share what she was feeling.

"All of these breakdowns have resulted from key decisions I made," she said meekly. "Maybe I'm the problem. Maybe I don't deserve to be on this team."

I looked across the executive team and saw that their faces were contorted in the same expression: confused disagreement. She didn't understand their reactions, so I used a closed question to clarify the group's response to her.

"Rachel," I said, " I'm going to ask a question to the group, and I want to make sure you take in their response. Okay?"

"Okay," she said.

Then I asked the group, "Would you please raise your hand if you feel Rachel does deserve to be on this team."

All the hands shot up enthusiastically, jolting Rachel out of her isolated experience and into connection with her peers. With a teary laugh and sigh of relief, her body relaxed. Everyone had a smile on their face.

The leader then said, "Stop trying to fire yourself already!" The whole room laughed, and a deep sameness pervaded the room.

Reframing

Reframing is a conceptual and verbal tool used to create flexibility, safety, and range in conversation. It is a very effective method for reducing differences or conflict. It involves changing how a person perceives, defines, or describes an experience.

Reframing helps us to see situations from a larger or more long-term perspective. It reduces implicit criticism or threatening language and shifts the emphasis in conversation from the negative to the positive or neutralizes the good and bad valence altogether. The use of reframes helps to create an atmosphere of safety and good faith. A good reframe can take the sting out and soften a perspective. Ultimately, it needs to work for the person whose communication was reframed, so we must always check their responsiveness to our offer.

Here are a few examples of reframes.

"I think he's an arrogant jerk" can be reframed as "You don't feel respected by him."

If your colleague says, "That was really chaotic," you can rephrase it as "That was playful and unpredictable."

A coaching client tells you, "I am a manipulator." You reframe a question: "Why are you working for your goals indirectly? What would happen if you were more direct?"

Reframing is a very valuable skill for lowering tension and creating sameness in conversations, but to become good at it requires a lot of practice.

Difference Skills

There is research that suggests that the best teams are composed of high performers who also enjoy their work and their team. We know that high-functioning teams cultivate commonality, psychological safety, and trust. Because their bonds run deep, they can explore ideas, express their doubts, reveal their mistakes, and offer challenges to their teammates.

Most importantly, they are not threatened by their differences. They understand that differences create growth and are necessary for good collaboration. An ability to explore our differences allows for our narrow perspectives to expand into greater ones that are wider, more inclusive, and allow for more complexity. But working with our differences requires embodied awareness so that we can move toward them rather than away from them.

Notice Differences

Differences are exciting to our nervous system; they create energy and heighten our perceptions. However, we are conditioned to minimize our differences because they easily become conflicts that can be damaging to relationships. So, we very quickly avoid, minimize, or soften them. The first step in learning to work with differences in a new way is to notice them and be curious about them. This means we must learn to acknowledge the impact differences have on our body, for better or worse, and override the interpretation that something is wrong.

Pay Attention to Impact

Rather than moving away from these sensations, become familiar with them. They are, after all, just dynamic sensations in the body. Through the use of mindfulness, you can notice their qualities and become friendlier toward them. This means actually feeling sensations like churning in the stomach, heat in the face and neck, jitteriness in the limbs, an impulse to cry in the face, and so on.

Then employ the bodily cues to bring the sensations to a manageable level. Give a cognitive reminder such as "These sensations are okay" or "There is nothing dangerous that I have to move away from." Employ a rhythmic breathing technique, lengthening the exhale. Allow yourself to feel your body's density and gravity's pressure against your form. Make supportive social contact when possible: soften your eyes and face, reflectively listen, and express appreciation for your opportunity to learn and practice.

Be Curious

When you feel present and grounded, turn toward exploring the difference. The most important cue in conversation is a safety cue. For example, "I am interested in our differences. I would like to compare notes about our respective opinions. Are you up for that?"

Getting permission is very helpful to others because they are given a choice. People will usually respond positively when we model curiosity and openness, are free of typical judgments, and ask for consent.

Then we just explore the differences like we are playing tennis. We take turns expressing our views, and we take turns listening. Listening and reflection will lower anxiety levels immediately. If we start to compete or move to dominate one another, our anxiety levels will go up. When that happens, a simple confession can be helpful. For example, "I notice some anxiety in my body right now, and I need a second to calm myself down." We use the reactivity to humble ourselves—not to blame others—and to disclose our own challenges. Remember that the autonomic nervous system is binary, so when it prepares to defend, it takes some initiative to bring it back to a resting state. When we both demonstrate listening, reflection, and mutual respect, our nervous systems will immediately respond.

Finally, remember when expressing our viewpoints, less is more. Simplicity and clarity are most valuable because listeners can easily receive our message. Ensure that speech is focused and congruent. Pay particular attention to the impact it has on the listener. Are they interested and attentive? Are they restless or withdrawn? Then we can learn to use our speech in a way that enlivens rather than drains or threatens others. But it takes practice and receptivity to feedback to hone this skill. Clarity of mind, calmness in the body, and simplicity of speech support the exploration of differences.

Exploring differences successfully requires new information and perspectives. Summarizing what we have heard and learned together will reestablish a sense of sameness as a conversation comes to a close, even when we don't agree.

Fundamental Openness

A healthy, dynamic balance of sameness and difference is required for our well-being, growth, and creativity. When our commonality is valued and cultivated, we feel safe, relaxed, coherent, and stable in our relationships. On the other hand, too much conformity leads to stagnation, boredom, and, paradoxically, passive-aggressiveness. Conflicts remain in the background because our differences are marginalized rather than explored. A group that is not allowed to differ is a group that is not allowed to grow, and life doesn't tolerate that.

Differences are exciting, creative, and life giving as they catalyze movement and lead our attention outside of what is familiar or known. But when our differences are not held in the reality of our sameness, our commonality, and our fundamental belonging, they often are anxiety provoking, threatening, and overwhelming. People naturally pull away, shut down, and become despondent when groups overemphasize differences.

Through Zen training, we cultivate the fundamental openness of awareness and presence. The more we connect with this openness, the less we cling to our preferences for sameness or difference. We can work easily with both. Essentially, we become braver in regard to the twists and turns of our experiences and the ups and downs of relationships. Training in sustained availability means we have access to more choices and, truthfully, better ones. We are able to choose loving-kindness, extend equanimity, and practice compassionate activity. Our life becomes one of devotion and wholeheartedness. But for this, we need to practice meditation and develop our interpersonal skills.

Openness, availability, and greater choice can express itself simply in conversation. I facilitated a conflict between coworkers, one Black and one White. The Black person asserted that empathy is impossible because of the differences in our history and racialized experiences. I noticed that I felt confined by a "truth" about our differences, and I did not want to challenge that assertion. But I steadied myself, extended my exhale, connected to fundamental openness, and offered another perspective.

I said, "I hear you believe your differences cannot be bridged, and from that perspective, talking about them isn't worth the risk because the conversation will, most likely, fail." I paused, then continued, "But I can't genuinely support that viewpoint because I know our capacity to empathize is profound, and our common humanity is deep. I want to ask you to try to see what happens. Are you willing?"

In fact, he shared and had a powerful exchange with his colleague rooted in reflective listening, questions, clear expressions, and reframes. The first level of sharing was coded in many narratives, such as "as a Black leader I need to be twice as good because very little grace will be afforded to me if I make a mistake." The White colleague reflected the content of what he heard, which he did well. However, he did not reflect the emotional undertones present in the communication. So, I asked him whether he heard any emotions or feelings from his coworker.

"I heard anger at the unfair and prejudiced standards he feels held to. I also heard resentment because I'm not held to those same standards." Based on the reflections, I noticed a quiet begin to settle in the speaker's nervous system. I checked if these emotions were present, and he said yes. I turned to the listener again and asked if he detected any other feelings.

"I noticed your voice tremble toward the end. I don't think it was the anger or resentment." Then he asked a question. "I wonder if you feel vulnerable in our team and, perhaps, even in our relationship?" This was a very genuine question and had a real impact on the speaker. The experience of being seen and heard by the listener created sameness between them and the whole team. The atmosphere of the conversation changed from mistrust to possibility and from separation to an embodied experience of connection. The doubt about the power of empathy dissolved.

There is a definition of love that says, "Love is that which enables choice." Responding from the ground of vast openness in our relationships is love, and it is the choice that moves us beyond fighting, fleeing, and freezing into an open field of possibility.

3

DEVELOPING EMOTIONAL MATURITY

Diane Musho Hamilton

The more we witness our emotional reactions and understand how they work, the easier it is to refrain. —Pema Chödrön

Emotional maturity is an aspect of adult development that refers to the awareness of emotions, the ability to regulate them, and success in communicating them. It means developing intimacy with sensations and feelings in the body and becoming familiar with corresponding thinking in the mind. Most importantly, it means seeing clearly how there is a feedback loop between thoughts and feelings, which can be interrupted so emotions are more easily managed.

As we mature, we learn to feel fully without dwelling on or drowning in our emotions. We learn to clarify their meanings and can freely choose between expressing them, holding them privately, or simply letting them go. We have far more freedom to decide, depending on circumstances and emotions' positive or negative effects on our communications. And because we know how to work with our emotions, we are more capable of being present to the emotional states of others.

Experiencing feelings and emotions is valuable because they are a form of intelligence. They carry information, life force, and energy. They connect us more fully to our bodies and, therefore, to each other. This connectedness means that we can communicate and share them, deepening our relationships in the presence of powerful states like grief, vulnerability, righteous anger, or fear. Emotions contribute to meaning and give depth to our experience as human beings.

We can all develop and mature emotionally. But we are deeply habituated by our disposition, inherited family traits, patterns, and how our culture of origin relates to emotions and their expression. Because of these differences in individual temperament and cultural conditioning, some of us feel too little, while others feel too much. Most of us have never been taught how to work with bodily sensations, feelings, or emotional states, let alone moods or deeper emotional processes like depression or grief. So, learning to be with our emotions and those of others is an essential dimension of any self-development or transformational practice.

While positive emotions are easier to experience for most people, the more negative, difficult, or painful emotions may harm us. Raw expressions of emotions such as anger, jealousy, or compulsive worrying can distort our thinking, shut down conversations, provoke resentment, or result in a complete breakup of relationships because they are energetically so impactful.

To mature our emotional lives, we must be interested in learning about emotions, their regulation, and expression. We must be willing to feel our bodies and watch what happens in our minds. Maturity means flexibility: letting go of emotional habits that don't serve us while allowing for feeling responses that are fresh and enlivening, such as new bouts of excitement, profound waves of sadness, or creative fits of jealousy. We must be prepared to be patient with this development because learning to work with our emotional states takes commitment, self-awareness, and lots of practice. It only happens over time.

Spectrum of Emotion

It is helpful to begin by making several distinctions about emotions. First, we need to practice identifying sensations in the body—for example, trembling in the hands, constriction in the throat, or pressure in the head. These sensations can be intense, chaotic, or just overwhelming to feel directly. Probably the most basic and important aspect of emotional work is to befriend the direct experience of bodily sensations.

People often use the word *feelings* to refer to bodily sensations. But our discussion will refer to feelings as sensations assigned an emotional label or a name such as fear, sadness, or anger. For example, churning in the solar plexus would be considered a feeling in our discussion if "anxious" or "distraught" is added to the description of that sensation of churning.

Emotions signify more complex psychological processes involving the feedback loop between the sensations in the body and thoughts in the mind. The thoughts we have in the wake of intense sensations and feelings—thoughts such as repeating the story of what caused the emotion, justifying ourselves, blaming others, and strategizing reactions—all fuel the feedback loop between body and mind, increasing the production of stress hormones, and often leading to negative behaviors. Emotions are this complex of body, mind, and behavioral interactions, and we must get to know our complex patterns to become more skilled in working with them.

We transition in the spectrum of emotion from *sensation* to *feeling* to *emotion* to *mood*. A mood is a sustained emotion. There may be thoughts or stories about our mood and why it persists, or the story may have disappeared. It is common to be unsure of what caused a mood. Moods feel less like weather and more like atmosphere; their energy impacts the people around us. People enjoy us when we are in a good mood but run away when a lousy mood approaches. Moods may naturally occur due to unexpected changes, dilemmas, or difficult life circumstances. But they can also result simply from habit or a choice to punish, withdraw, or even communicate indirectly intentionally.

Remember that no sensation, feeling, emotion, or mood is inherently negative. Painful maybe, or intense perhaps, but not necessarily destructive. The problem is that much of our emotional lives is born of habit, and sometimes the things we say or do because of our emotional states create negativity in our lives. So, learning how to acknowledge and feel emotions and moods and how to release them is essential in developing emotional maturity. Generally speaking, we need to feel more fully and release more readily.

The sustained quality of emotions and moods forms the basis for an emotional *state* becoming a personality *trait*.[1] In their purest form, emotions are like the weather. They should blow through our body-mind unobstructed and dissipate easily. Young children provide good examples of how feelings are temporary state experiences that arrive, bloom, and can vanish quickly. They show us how to inhabit feelings without dwelling on or getting stuck in them. Children's feelings move quickly because the thinking mind, which has not yet matured, does not elaborate or complexify them. As adults, our thinking, storytelling mind helps keep sensations and feelings alive.

When emotions are more deeply entrained in the mind and body and have become a trait, an attitude, or a characteristic, as in "an angry person" or "a confused soul," they have undue influence on our behaviors, actions, and relationships. But no matter how established they have become, we can engage in a practice that will loosen their grip, allowing for more freedom and flow.

Feeling Fully, Letting Go

When I went to Naropa Institute, I wanted to learn to meditate and experience more peace in my life. I didn't imagine that more peace meant a deeper dive into what I was actually feeling and thinking. I thought I should simply ignore my feelings, quiet my mind, and behave well. But that was naive. First, I couldn't ignore them, and second, I learned that when we bypass our feelings and emotions, we lose contact with energy and life force. We fail to acknowledge their innate intelligence and ignore the truth of our experience. I was introduced to a practice called the transmutation of emotion, and it reminds me of certain kinds of military training where you are introduced to the experience of panic so that you can access clear thinking and deliberate action when panic inevitably occurs.

Each of us has the capacity to feel and emote, as well as the ability to ignore sensations, feelings, and thoughts. So, this is a practice we can all develop. The transmutation of emotion is learning to use both abilities more deliberately. We usually have a favorite strategy for avoiding painful sensations, such as dulling them with food or drink, self-medicating with drugs, channel surfing, shopping, scrolling on our phone, or just thinking instead of feeling. So, we must return to the beginning and learn about what is occurring in our body and mind.

The first step in developing more emotional maturity is the same for everyone. When we experience a strong emotional reaction, we must stop and place our attention exclusively on our body, focusing on the sensations directly. We use the same process if we cannot locate feelings or sensations. When we attend to bodily sensations and breathe gently, evenly, and rhythmically, and while exploring, the body and mind become more coherent. If we can't locate feelings, we need to be patient. They will come. If we are strong feelers, intensity can be modulated by focusing lightly on the breath and the feeling. If we also suspend our thoughts, we will gain more confidence in our ability to feel.

At first, it is challenging to hit pause on our thoughts and interpretations. To make it easier, we suggest sitting or lying down to quiet the mind, focusing attention directly on the body, simply experiencing what is present and noticing how the sensations shift or change. It is helpful to hold attention broadly on the body, letting it move about, noting active sensations and places of rest or calm. (A condensed set of instructions for working with the sensations and emotions is included at the end of this chapter.)

I had an experience of the usefulness of this practice when my son developed a mental illness during the pandemic. He started hearing voices, and for me, it was something I had never imagined or prepared for. So, I felt truly terrified much of the time. Willie has Down syndrome and is thirty-four now. He wasn't sleeping very well during the isolation of the pandemic, combined with sleep apnea. He started to hear the voices coming out of the radio. They were menacing, often tormenting and taunting him.

He was diagnosed with unspecified psychosis. My nervous system was in complete overload. I felt terrified and constantly frustrated because it was impossible to get an appointment with a psychotherapist, let alone a psychiatrist, for months. I was required to work more closely with my ex-husband to get Willie into treatment, which wasn't easy either. My son was scared and bewildered by what was happening, and once he became totally overwhelmed and had to go to the emergency room. Sometimes, I was so flooded by feeling that all I could do was cry. So, I picked up the practice of transmuting the emotions, knowing it would help me.

I can't believe how often I was coping with my emotions rather than feeling them. Eventually, I had the wherewithal to notice I was overwhelmed or frozen with fear. I would take time to just lie down on my bed and feel everything. Coming to stillness, I immediately encountered dark thoughts about the future. Images of asylums and overcrowded mental health facilities would flood my awareness, and the sad, distant look of my disabled son, who didn't seem to know me any longer, would haunt me. Remembering that we often think and imagine to avoid feeling, I would intentionally pause these distressing images and thoughts, bringing my full attention to the present and the swirling sensations in my body. I would breathe gently and evenly, just feeling the sensations. Sometimes I would cry.

And when my mind wandered, I returned to the body. Mostly, I would feel everything as precisely as possible: the heat in my face, throbbing in my head, and trembling in my limbs. There was nausea in my gut, a tense, set jaw, and a contracted inability to take a deep breath. Then, I would start to name the feelings as I understood them: terror, dread, overwhelm, frustration, anger, helplessness. Simply naming the feelings helped put my mind further to rest because they made total sense. Who wouldn't be feeling what I was feeling? I also refused to be distracted by ideas of what I should be doing to care for Willie. I knew I was doing everything I could.

There was always a moment when the intensity of the sensations would subside, and I would relax. At the same time, my heart seemed to open, and kindness for Willie, his father, and myself bloomed. This experience put me in touch with my underlying resilience and the capacity of my heart to deal with life's challenges. Because of my training in the practice of tonglen from the Tibetan Buddhist tradition (see chapter 18 in *Everything Is Workable*[2]), in my mind I would extend this kindness to every family who was experiencing the stress of the pandemic and the pain of mental illness. It was a great reminder that we are not alone in our suffering and that our hearts are big enough to include others.

In working with my fear about Willie's psychosis, as I said, I didn't need to work too much with my cognition because I was thinking constantly throughout each day about how best to care for him. I just needed to hit pause on the dark-future thoughts and simply feel more fully, allowing the body's intelligence to guide me. But there are many times when our thinking mind interacts with our sensations, making the transmutation more difficult. Emotions, as we said, involve the feedback loop between sensations in the body and the thoughts in our heads about those sensations.

An example of a more typical scenario of working with emotions could be a conflict at work. Imagine for a moment that during a meeting, a colleague disagreed with your opinion on a proposal. And then imagine that your boss seemed to side with your colleague without fully listening to the strengths of your idea. We have all had exchanges at work where we didn't feel fully understood.

Imagine that this exchange created agitation in you for the rest of the day. It remained unresolved, and you were still upset when you finally arrived home from work. But rather than feeling the experience fully, you keep playing the scenario over in your head, feeling irritation with your colleague and disappointment in your boss. You tell the story to your partner, but it doesn't do anything to alleviate your distress. This would be a perfect time to employ the transmutation process. When emotions are fresh and meaningful, they provide the ideal opportunity to explore.

First, find a quiet spot to sit or lie down and then sink into the sensations. When working with powerful emotions, we often experience chaos or overwhelm when focusing on the body. So, begin by feeling the whole experience, moving between thoughts, feelings, and sensations.

Then, focus specifically on what is happening in your body, hitting pause on your thoughts. You keep noticing and questioning the sensations. What is their texture, temperature, movement, and scale? Are they continuous, or do they change? On a scale of 1 to 10, how unpleasant are they? What makes them unpleasant? Stay curious and keep breathing gently, staying present to them.

After exploring the sensations directly, you begin to name them as feelings. Some are predictable, such as frustration, hurt, or even betrayal, but others are surprising, such as powerlessness, jealousy, or apathy. You suspend any judgments you may have about yourself for having these feelings. After five or ten minutes, the attention on your body and use of the breath creates coherence between body and mind, and you will experience a definite sensation of calming down.

When relaxation sets in, it is time to bring cognition back online by asking yourself a golden question: "What is right about this emotion?" This inquiry can be risky because there is always a danger that the negative thoughts will take over again and drive more unpleasant feelings. But when coherence is reestablished, thinking will often become productive again. The threats to our self-image dissipate, and some helpful thoughts become available—for example, "I see value in my proposal, and I want to ensure others understand it"; "I want to collaborate with my colleagues rather than compete with them, and

I wonder how best to do that"; and "I have responses to offer to the critique, and I would like an opportunity to respond."

According to Buddhist tradition, when we work with transmutation by suspending thought for a time, emotion is freed from the ego's grip and its wisdom becomes clear. Anger transmutes to clarity, and sorrow turns to compassion. Confusion becomes spaciousness, while fear puts us into contact with our vitality. This is why we set the story aside while practicing feeling and then ask, "What is right?" about the emotion. Both liberate the mind from egoic clinging and defensiveness and allow more positive responses to emerge.

Working with emotions is a holistic, nonlinear experience, so while the transmutation of emotion provides a linear structure, the order of these steps might only sometimes work. Some people experience much louder thoughts, while bodily sensations capture others. So, give yourself permission to explore the steps, finding a sequence that works for you. But remember, using the breath to regulate intensity is a crucial element of experiencing the sensations, and interrupting the feedback loop is essential to recalibrating the nervous system.

Finally, what to do with moods? The transmutation of emotion exercise can also be helpful in the case of a problematic mood. It will help us feel the sensations and identify the thoughts that keep the mood going. We can often discover the cause of the mood and how to better relate with our body and mind. There may be a communication that needs to happen that we have been trying to avoid. (Please see *Everything Is Workable* for a fuller discussion on communication skills.[3])

If the mood is particularly dense, we need to create a physical state change. This can involve engaging in an activity involving the senses, such as listening to music, dancing, or taking a shower. Getting outside, breathing the fresh air, or walking will change the state. Exercise is an excellent state-changing activity. So is meditation. People often rely on alcohol to alter their mood, which, if occasional, is fine. But as we know, if it becomes a habit, it will ultimately erode well-being.

Positive Emotional Traits

The purpose of our practice is to give space to emotions, receiving their information, energy, and life force, allowing them to dissolve naturally, and unhooking them from destructive actions. Only pure, open awareness remains when an emotion or mood has been released. Open awareness is not a state because it doesn't come and go. It is the field in which all emotions arise. We refer to pure awareness as ever present, indestructible, and timeless. Meditation allows us to experience awareness directly and to discover its vast, boundless nature, free of judgments, preconceptions, biases, and opinions.

When the mind rests in this open stillness, it is the perfect time to cultivate positive emotional states such as loving-kindness, compassion, joyfulness, and equanimity. Any practice that engenders a positive emotional state in us, free of egoic clinging and attachment, is beneficial. If we practice these states, they will eventually become traits. Again, when we have access to pure, open awareness, it is the best time to invoke the positive states because nobody likes a happy face pasted over worry or kindness driven by the need to be acknowledged. We can all feel and see it, and we mostly don't like it.

In the Buddhist tradition, the Four Immeasurables are studied and practiced. Loving-kindness is the expression of benevolence, friendliness, amity, goodwill, and active interest in others. The feeling tone is warm, open-hearted, and caring. Compassion is the willingness to feel others' pain and suffering. It differs from empathy in that, according to brain science, no distress signal exists in the brain.[4] It is expressed in many ways but is characterized by a willingness to help. Sympathetic joy is a positive response to the good fortune of others, allowing their happiness, good fortune, and luck to become an enhancement to one's own joy. Equanimity is the capacity to experience the ups and downs in life in equal measure. One learns to be calm, patient, and accommodating of whatever occurs in life.

In addition to the Four Immeasurables, gratitude, or the ability to be thankful for our life, is one of the most valuable positive emotions.

This includes demonstrating appreciation for others and returning their goodwill. On the other hand, forgiveness allows us to adapt when hurt or offended. As a character trait, one may become more forgiving, capable of releasing many everyday offenses.

We also value fun, playfulness, and a sense of humor in our practice. Sitting allows these qualities to arise naturally, and since they are contagious, they contribute to the joy in the community and the bond we have created. Nothing is more satisfying than a good laugh in a group of people who enjoy humor, especially the willingness to laugh at oneself.

To sum up, an emotionally mature person has cultivated an intimacy and understanding of their feelings. They see how much emotions embellish and give meaning to life, and they learn to be responsible for and accountable to them. They experience the fullness of positive and negative emotions but have much more freedom and choice about how and when they are expressed.

Because they are intimate with their experience, they can give words to what they are feeling and include feelings in their communications. They appreciate the emotions of others, are not scared by feeling capacity, intensity, or vulnerability, and have confidence in their and our inherent resilience. They can serve as models for what emotional maturity looks and feels like, using their emotional intelligence to cultivate and deepen positive states, inspiring all of us to develop ourselves in this way.

Transmutation of Emotion Practice

Take time this week to simply notice and be willing to feel sensations and study emotional states as they arise. Begin by feeling the overall experience of the emotion, including bodily sensations, feelings, and thoughts in the mind.

1. *Focus specifically on the sensations in the body.* What sensations are present? Notice particular parts of the body: your

stomach, solar plexus, heart, throat, jaw, et cetera. Pay attention to the difference in sensations and note whether they are pleasant or unpleasant. Allow yourself to feel sensations like swirling, gripping, aching, vibrating, and how they move and change. If the sensations are too chaotic or overwhelming, focus lightly on the breath, allowing natural inhalation and extending the exhale to help decrease the intensity of the experience.

2. *Name the feelings.* Naming the different feelings will help you validate and clarify the entire emotional experience. If you can, come up with multiple labels for the feelings. Notice the impact of naming them. Does naming change the experience of the sensations in any way? Notice that you may experience multiple feelings simultaneously, such as anger, hurt, and vulnerability.

3. *Pay attention to the full emotional process.* Observe the body/mind feedback loop closely. Notice how thoughts reinforce the sensations in the body and how sensations stimulate thoughts. This feedback loop is what gives rise to a full-blown emotion, and this is what causes prolonged emotions.

4. *Hit pause on the story.* This step involves suspending the thoughts and storyline about the emotion and simply feeling the body again. This step interrupts the feedback loop so the body can return to a resting state. Mental activity helps us avoid discomfort in the body. So, it takes practice to put the mind on "pause" and bring the attention back to the body. The mind quiets by stepping out of the narrative and the body begins to recalibrate. Use the breath to help decrease intensity. Feel the energy of the emotional experience directly and notice the aliveness of the emotion.

5. *Ask yourself, "What is right about this emotion?"* Now that the mind is quiet and the body is beginning to calm down, you can ask, "What is right about these feelings or this emotion?" Notice whether your cognition has changed. Have

your thoughts become more compassionate and more help-ful? Can you trust your thinking again?

6. *Let it all go.* Allow the thoughts, feelings, and sensations to subside. Remember that it takes time for stress hormones to clear out of the bloodstream. Sometimes, letting go is difficult, so "letting be" may be a good step before "letting go" is possible.

4

SHADOW

Gabriel Kaigen Wilson

Shadow work is the way to illumination.—Carl Jung

Those drawn to meditation seek relief from pain and entry to enlightenment, wisdom, and compassion. Meditation is the tried-and-true method in the Buddhist tradition for reducing suffering, enhancing well-being, and providing a basis for ethical training and concern for others. While meditation is effective in preparing the mind for psychological work, it doesn't directly address the patterns in the psyche that are often the source of pain or wounding that perpetuate suffering and block our growth.

Ken Wilber has identified four dimensions that an integrally informed spiritual practice should include. The first is spiritual and involves practices like meditation or prayer, wherein one cultivates spiritual awakening or identifies with something greater than oneself. The second is physical. He asserts that physical training creates a more powerful container for spiritual realization. The third is the development of cognition and helpful mental maps. Spiritual training involves studying and developing a clear understanding of Buddhist teachings (or other spiritual truths). Integral theory, applied to spiritual practice, can help us navigate our interior reality and the externals of the world around us. Finally, he advocates for the role of psychology in our practice. Most importantly, he promotes the exploration of shadow as an essential contribution from the analytic psychology of Carl Jung.

For Jung, the word *shadow* represents the unconscious or hidden parts of the psyche. It points to any content that cannot be held in the light of awareness because it is painful, socially unacceptable, or contrary to one's conscious identity. This content is, therefore, ignored, suppressed, or denied. One of the most potent discoveries of Western psychology is that under certain circumstances, a person's unwanted impulses, feelings, and qualities are disowned but then projected onto others.

Ken Wilber directly discusses the phenomenon of projection when he frames the shadow as any part of the psyche that cannot be identified as "I." Instead, it is projected outward as "you," "he," "she," "them," "it," or "its." For example, "I am not angry, you are." Or "I am not greedy, they are."

Robert Masters, a former spiritual teacher who became a psychotherapist, defines shadow as "the place within each of us that contains what we don't know, don't like, or deny about ourselves. Our shadow holds our unattended and not-yet-illuminated conditioning—all the programmed ways we act, think, feel, and choose without knowing why."[1]

Shadow work is devoted to recovering those parts of ourselves that we have marginalized or projected onto others. Jung, Wilber, and Masters agree that integrating the shadow involves acknowledging and transmuting these hidden aspects of the self. So, shadow work involves looking directly at the parts of ourselves that we don't like. It is essential in becoming self-aware and manifesting one's complete, whole self. But spiritual practice generates shadow material because shining light exclusively on our deepest nature will leave other parts of the psyche in the dark.

Spiritual Bypassing

A second psychological concept important in cultivating a spiritual practice is the notion of *spiritual bypassing*, a term coined by the psychologist John Welwood. Spiritual bypassing "is the use of spiritual practices and beliefs to avoid dealing with our painful feelings, unresolved wounds, and developmental needs."[2] The greater our desire to avoid pain, the more likely we are to use spiritual beliefs and practices to bypass the sources of our suffering.[3]

I have experienced this firsthand. After I graduated from college, I became very close to a group of ten fellow graduates. We developed deep bonds based on our conviction that the best way to address the confusion, consumerism, and corruption in the world was a radical commitment to raising consciousness. We became obsessed with awakening, exploring the spiritual marketplace, sampling different meditation retreats, and trying out various methods. I remember it as an intellectually enlightening time as we posed questions, compared notes, and discussed our experiences. I was also very excited that my longing for a meaningful community had been met.

We didn't understand then, however, that each of us retained unprocessed wounds and historical pain that affected our relationships and informed our decision-making. The list included losing parents at a young age; growing up in abusive households; encountering serious health challenges such as cancer or, in my case, heart arrhythmia; problems with substance abuse; and mental illness. These experiences brought us together as a community needing healing, and our pain gave rise to our spiritual longings.

I became interested in Welwood's notion of spiritual bypassing because our forays into spiritual practice made us worse human beings. We began as friends who lived near one another. We did things together, held potluck dinners, and watched movies on the weekends. We shared ideas, laughed, and enjoyed each other's company.

But as we embarked on these spiritual quests, our goodwill toward one another plummeted, and our communications became fraught and painful. We carelessly shared feedback that was harsh and unkind. One group member now seemed subject to fits of rage, yelling, "None of you can hear the truth" or "You aren't capable of authentic communication." I remember being appalled by what I was seeing and hearing from him. Ironically, he was the person who decided he was ready to be a teacher after only a couple of retreats.

Our healthy boundaries collapsed, making the relationships emotionally enmeshed and physically messy. People ate one another's food without asking and borrowed clothes without permission, and no one seemed to care. At the same time, there was a substantial increase in drug use, including weed, mushrooms, alcohol, and MDMA. This led to decreased rationality, a strong character trait the group had formerly shared. Premonitions, intuitive guesses, and magical thinking now replaced common sense.

I began to break away from the group when my closest friend suffered a severe psychotic break, and my other friends offered interpretations that had no basis in reality or mental health research. Their responses to his condition sounded like spiritual babble to my ear. I started to feel alienated from these friendships. During this time, I picked up Robert Master's book *Spiritual Bypassing*, and as I read, the light bulb above my head switched on. He writes,

> Some of the signs of spiritual bypassing are an exaggerated detachment, emotional numbing, and repression, overemphasis on the positive, anger-phobia, blind or overly tolerant compassion, weak or porous boundaries, lopsided development, e.g., cognitive intelligence often being far ahead of emotional and moral intelligence, debilitating judgment about one's negativity or shadow side, devaluation of the personal relative to the spiritual, and delusions of having arrived at a higher level of being.[4]

This long, thoughtful list explained my experience and sobered me up. I began recognizing a profound and somewhat puzzling relationship between psychological-emotional work and spiritual practice. I was deeply affected by this and left with many questions. Ken Wilber's writing helped me clarify these questions, particularly in my life. His integral theory throws a wide net over the vast array of human knowledge, integrating many perspectives, from psychology to spirituality, but also including science, art, philosophy, and culture. He forms a coherent conceptual framework that makes very useful distinctions for those seeking clarity on these issues.

One crucial distinction he offers is that the goal and method of meditation and psychotherapy differ. The purpose of meditation is to dis-identify with what arises in awareness. This detachment allows for the complete identification with being or awareness itself, which is inherently fulfilling and free from ordinary life's perpetual ups and downs. "Transcendence," he says, "has long been defined as a process of dis-identification."

But rather than *dis-identify* with objects in the mind, psychotherapy *identifies* with the content of consciousness, including the desires and aversions of the self, the psychodynamic storytelling about family and friends, the narrative arc of dreams, and all the intriguing dramas of love, life, and work, including the emotional impact on our psyche and the quality of our relationships. This is at the heart of psychological work.

These mental patterns are not relinquished in psychotherapy but explored in depth, albeit in different ways. They are acknowledged, analyzed, interpreted, reframed, elaborated, or refined to make a friendlier relationship with oneself and one's world. Only the patterns seen as destructive to well-being by therapist and client alike are relinquished. The rest of them remain in play, and the mind doesn't come to rest like it does in meditation.

Again, meditation does the opposite. Attachments to all phenomena, perspectives, and patterns in the body-mind are acknowledged and released. Ken gives a simple, everyday example for us to consider. He asks, "When something happens in life that makes you mad, do you identify with the anger or not? Do you acknowledge and express it, or dis-identify with it and let it go?" He says it all depends.[5]

"If my anger arises in awareness and is authentically experienced and owned as *my* anger, *then* the goal is to continue dis-identification." He then goes on to say, "But if *my* anger arises in awareness and is experienced as *your* anger or *his* anger or *its* anger—but not *my* anger—the goal is to first identify with and re-own the anger. But if that re-ownership of (the anger) in shadow is not first undertaken, then meditation on anger simply increases the alienation—meditation becomes 'transcend and deny,' which is exactly unhealthy development."[6] This distinction explains why experienced meditators may still struggle in relationships, are subject to ethical lapses, and display neurotic patterns that puzzle their friends.

Individual Shadow Work

Shadow work incorporates unconscious material by bringing it into the light of awareness. Or by exploring what appears as "not me" and discovering how "it is me." When we recognize our shadow material as part of the self, the energy bound up by the effort to keep it out of awareness is freed up. People completing shadow work will often laugh, giggle, and smile, their eyes lighting up in recognition of themselves. At other times, they cry because it is poignant, even embarrassing, to re-own our projections. Almost always, a powerful experience of compassion or empathy arises.[7]

Our ability to convert shadow into wisdom and turn trapped energy into compassionate activity is truly remarkable. We become more whole and integrated. It is easier to confess our errors, receive negative feedback without defensiveness, and get off the seesaw of self-idealization and self-denigration. We become more stable, human, and real.

Shadow work magically frees us of the emotional entanglement with others, clearing the lens so that we see people on their own terms, complete with the characteristics we love and those we don't. Shadow work doesn't change others. It simply allows us to be more intimate with ourselves. As we do, we are free to accept or reject the complexity and challenges of others without undue distress. There can be very positive outcomes of integrating shadow. The identities we least want to claim can bring energy, life force, and joy to our lives. It is a strange alchemy, but here is a story that illustrates this idea.

A student of Roshi's, who I'll name Gil, was reaching a milestone in his training. Like in the martial arts, Zen students undergo challenges to demonstrate the fruits of their practice through live interactions and questioning by other community members. The purpose of the public ceremony is for the aspirant to demonstrate their ability to go beyond ordinary conceptual thinking and demonstrate deeper Zen understanding. When the student successfully completes this challenge, they advance to the status of a senior practitioner.

The ceremony required preparation, and Gil was readying himself for it. He had focused his attention and invigorated his zazen and koan study, traveling from South America to spend time in Utah with Roshi. But the pandemic hit several months before the ceremony was to take place. He had to fly home to Colombia immediately before the borders closed, and Roshi had to postpone the ceremony indefinitely. You can imagine how frustrating that must have been after all the work he had put in.

They resumed their online practice, but over the course of several months, Roshi noticed something in Gil had changed. Before, Gil had been fully present in his practice and study. Now, he seemed to have stopped following through on his commitments. During their weekly koan practice, he showed up without having prepared. The first time this happened, Roshi did not make anything of it. But when it happened again, she said, "What is happening with your practice?"

"What do you mean?" Gil said, perplexed.

"I'm noticing that since you went home, you seem to have lost momentum. When you were in the States, your commitment was on fire; I could see and feel your devotion. Now, it has faded. I know it has been frustrating to have to postpone the ceremony, especially because we don't know when it will happen."

He agreed and lamented his early return to Colombia. He said he had lost momentum and was suffering from uncertainty and the inability to stay focused. After listening to his account of his disappointment, she went on.

"I can totally understand how that would have happened. The uncertainty of the pandemic makes it difficult to continue in the same way. But I see a different quality in you that goes beyond the disappointment and disorientation. I detect a rebelliousness in you that I haven't seen before." The conversation took a bright turn. It was a moment when the feedback energized and heightened everyone's senses because something in the background was brought to the foreground. So, Roshi asked Gil to be curious about it rather than defensive.

"Would you be willing to identify with the rebel in you and explore him? He may be bringing something to the practice that is revitalizing, exciting even. Would you reflect on this voice and tell me what you discover in our meeting next week?"

Roshi didn't instruct him to let this identification go and fly right. She didn't point to how this identity had no fixed nature. For her, it was important for Gil first to locate this rebellious pattern, particularly because he was a firstborn son who was usually dutiful and diligent in his practice. She wanted to spend time with this shadow part of him.

Gil took her invitation to heart and asked himself, "As the rebel, where am I acting out in my life?" Surprisingly, different scenarios popped one after another like popcorn into his head. His whole identity shifted to see so many rebellious moments, from small things such as not responding to people's text messages right away to a recent time he evaded the cops. He rode his motorcycle and made an illegal maneuver. When a cop turned on his flashing lights and followed him, Gil kept going instead of pulling over! Eventually, he did pull over, and they immediately impounded his bike. He had to pay quite a bit to get it out of hock the next day.

He even called a friend to get his opinion on this matter. When he asked the friend whether he thought Gil was rebellious, the friend burst out laughing.

"You must be kidding me?! Your whole lifestyle is rebellious, especially your pursuit of Zen!"

Once Gil made contact with this part of himself, consciously owning it, he returned to Roshi with his reflections. They laughed together as he recounted all of his insights, especially when he told the story of outrunning the cops on his motorcycle.

"It's worse than I thought," she joked. "I was pretty sure there was a rebel in there," she said. "But I never expected that! Be careful, or you will get arrested, and I won't bail you out! And let's be clear. I am not asking the rebel to behave himself and disappear. But when you come to koan study, you must tell me who I am meeting with—the dutiful koan student or that rascally rebel. Either way is good with me. But I want to know who shows up so we are on the same page."

Roshi responded to Gil without reprimanding or shaming him because of her familiarity with shadow work. She paid attention to what the rebel's identity brought to their conversation. She noticed that Gil became energized and interested in this identity. He followed up and explored it, and it brought life force to their meetings.

As Ken has pointed out, this exploration would not have happened within the context of traditional Zen practice. But in the West, because of our familiarity with psychology, shadow work has a place in practice. Even though Roshi is not a psychotherapist, she is an integralist. So, she followed her intuition and brought this identity forward from the shadows. And it seemed to give everyone joy, except the police! Gil's disappointment in going home, the uncertainty of the pandemic, and the lockdown all gave rise to a quality of consciousness that could make it through anything. The rebel had intelligence and life force when Gil himself felt down and out. And the creative possibility that he could be affirmed and integrated is precisely the wonder of shadow work. And as a Zen practitioner, when the time is right, he can easily relinquish this identity into the vast, unconditioned nature of enlightened awareness far beyond duty and rebelliousness.

Golden Shadow

Over the years, I have listened as students describe their first encounter with Musho Roshi. I have heard everything from "All of a sudden, there was a glow around her" to "When I first saw her walking across the room, I knew she was going to change my life." Musho Roshi is a compelling figure, and she is a great teacher, but some of these descriptions strike me as otherworldly and remind me of my confusing time with my college friends.

But after learning about the shadow, I see we also project positive, disowned aspects of ourselves onto others as readily as we project our unwanted parts. This phenomenon is called the *Golden Shadow*. Our spiritual teachers, mentors, and friends can hold these positive qualities and aspirations for us. But owning these projections and asking how they also belong to us, or how we might cultivate them, is an example of working with the Golden Shadow.

Recently, a fellow Zen student named Rachel shared with me that she admired another student's ability to speak and express the teachings. I found this interesting because my experience of Rachel is that she communicates beautifully. This piqued my curiosity about Golden Shadow, so I asked her to describe what she appreciates in this friend in detail.

She said, "Gosh, I love the ease and joy she speaks with. She is really dynamic in front of a group. She starts with a joke and gets the whole room laughing. Then, she recites a poem from memory that opens everyone's heart. Then, she reveals a moment of awkward self-consciousness and lets it go in the next breath. And finally, she ends by guiding a powerful meditation."

"And if you were to give this set of characteristics an identity, what would you call it?" I asked.

"Easeful, joyful expression," she said. It seemed to me that this part of Rachel was in shadow. I could see it in her, but she couldn't see it in herself.

From here, I asked Rachel if she could find the easeful, joyful expressiveness in herself. After a few breaths, she giggled and said, "When I write. I love feeling myself in the act of writing. I relax and connect deeply. Novelty and insight that I didn't know were there spontaneously erupt. It is delightful! I make contact with vitality and creativity in writing. I wonder if I can bring it to my speaking."

I replied, "Of course you can, because it is already part of you."

Shadow Practice

Step 1: Face It

Using a journal, focus on an exceptionally provocative negative quality of a person. Describe the quality in vivid detail using the pronouns "he/him," "she/her," "they/them/it," and so forth. This is your opportunity to vent. In doing so, explore your experience fully, mainly what bothers you. Don't minimize anything. Take the opportunity to describe the disturbance as fully as possible and what is wrong with it.

Step 2: Talk to It

Now, enter into a dialogue in your journal, and talk directly with this quality as though it is a character, using the pronouns "you/yours." For example, if you are working with anger as the shadow quality, address the anger as though it were a person. This is your opportunity to make a relationship with the shadow. You may ask questions such as Who are you? Where do you come from? What do you want from me? What do you need to tell me? What gift are you bringing me? Then, allow the disturbing quality to respond to you. Allow yourself to be surprised by what emerges in the dialogue.

Step 3: Be It

Now, writing or speaking using the pronoun "I," become the person with this negative quality, and write about what it's like to be you using "I/me/mine." See the world entirely from the perspective of the one inhabiting this quality. Describe what it's like to be you. What do you see? Why are you here? What's right about you?*

Note: This version of shadow work was developed by Ken Wilber and his colleagues at the Integral Institute.

5

PURPOSE AND PRESENCE

Diane Musho Hamilton

The purpose of life is not to be happy. It is to be useful, to be honorable, to be compassionate, to have it make some difference that you have lived and lived well. —Ralph Waldo Emerson

I began meditating when I was twenty-two, and I practiced consistently for six years before recognizing I wasn't destined for a lifetime of retreat. I completed my degree in Buddhist psychology at Naropa University when I was twenty-four, and shortly after, at the invitation of a friend, I went to India and Nepal to study and practice with some of the Tibetan masters in the lineage of Chöygam Trungpa Rinpoche. I was fortunate to sit with Dilgo Khyentse Rinpoche, participate in elaborate ceremonies with Kalu Rinpoche, and listen to daily talks with Chökyi Nyima Rinpoche and Khenchen Thrangu Rinpoche.

But after six months in Asia, I came home. It was incredibly moving to be in the presence of such profound teachers, but I realized that the practice had to take root in my daily life, in the American context, and as a lay practitioner. I was not cut out to be a renunciate because I wasn't very religious. But I had received immeasurable guidance from the Three Treasures of the Buddhadharma, and it had become the unshakable foundation of my spiritual life. But my path would have to unfold in the culture and landscape of my home back in the United States.

This decision also meant I would have to make a living. I would strive to apply the teachings and practice into my work, hopefully without missionary zeal, so no one in the secular work world would notice. But how to make a living? Like many young people, I had been coached to "ask for what I wanted" or "follow my bliss," but neither of those instructions had helped clarify my direction. One day, I decided to change the question, and rather than asking, "What do I want?" I asked, "What are people telling me that I do well?"

After posing the new question, three conflicts arose, just like in a fairy tale. The first one was between my mother and brother. The second time, an argument erupted between friends, and a third conflict broke out in a twenty-person group trying to make a decision. Each time, I listened and helped them negotiate a solution to their dispute. Each time afterward, like in myth, someone approached me and thanked me for the help.

I was living in Seattle at the time. One afternoon, I walked by the Seattle Dispute Resolution Center and noticed an advertisement for a staff position. Prior to that moment, I had no concept of a mediator or idea that a dispute resolution center even existed. But I walked in and applied. I got the job and learned the fundamentals of mediation during my time there. Later, I returned to Utah and was hired as the director of Alternative Dispute Resolution for the Utah Courts, a newly created position.

Mediation is an expression of Buddhadharma in action. Both meditation and mediation are grounded in the truth of our fundamental unity. Meditators think they practice to attain it, but it is already here. Sitting still, we let go to experience it. Mediators think they bring people together, but more importantly, they reveal, point out, and use their commonalities and shared interests. Were this not the case, we would never enjoy the great peace of nonseparation, nor would wisdom and compassion naturally inform our lives. Both sustained meditation and successful mediation depend on recognizing, cultivating, and allowing inherent unity to function.

Jung and Calling

Carl Jung, the Swiss psychiatrist and successor to Sigmund Freud in analytical psychology, introduced the notion of individuation as the process of becoming one's true, unique self. Interestingly, he differentiated himself from his mentor, Freud, by moving beyond the focus on mental-emotional fixations and conflicts in the psyche to include the quest for meaning, self-realization, and spiritual transcendence.

For Jung, the call is an inner prompting that catalyzes individuation. It requires stepping into the unknown and committing to self-discovery, including facing fears and unresolved issues. The call may result in a calling—a specific lifestyle, career, or life purpose that one feels they were meant to do. The calling is ingrained in religious traditions, and the term is also used in a secular context, associating it with a strong inner desire or conviction about a particular career or life path.

In his book *The Soul's Code: In Search of Character and Calling*, James Hillman, the late Jungian psychoanalyst, suggests that orienting to calling reenchants our lives with beauty, mystery, and myth. He points out that cultures throughout history have identified the calling but used different names to describe it. The Romans named it *genius*; the Greeks, *daimon*; the Christians, *guardian angel*; the Neoplatonists, *ochema*. In Egypt, it was called the *ka* or *ba*, while the Eskimos and other people with shamanic traditions refer to the *free-soul* or *breath-soul*.[1] In Middle English, the word *calling* was used to refer to a vocation or profession, and it evolved from the Old Norse word *kalla*, meaning "to call" or "to summon."[2]

Hillman outlines the practical implications of heeding the call. First, we must recognize it as a legitimate fact of human existence. Second, to access beauty and enchantment, we must align our life with it. Third, we must see our history differently, realizing that accidents, including injury, heartache, and encounters with loss and death, are dimensions of our calling. Hillman says that callings can be postponed, avoided, or ignored, but he suggests that yielding to the call is ultimately life enhancing.

Iain McGilchrist, a psychiatrist, writer, and former Oxford literary scholar, offers a helpful distinction in reflecting upon calling or life purpose. He delineates between an intrinsic and extrinsic purpose. Intrinsic purpose reflects our innate gifts and talents, while our extrinsic purpose depends on the needs of our environment, conditions, and opportunities. Ideally, our intrinsic purpose lines up with extrinsic purpose. For example, before 1990, the innate talents of sharing oneself, one's passions, or one's expertise certainly existed. But computers were brand-new, nobody made videos, and YouTube, TikTok, and Instagram didn't exist. Now there is a calling referred to as "influencer" and a proliferation of them all over the internet because the external conditions allow for a completely new and different form of self-expression.

Upon completing graduate school, where Gabe had studied education policy and leadership, he had no job prospects. A mentor suggested he ask his classmates, friends, and colleagues what skills they most appreciated in him. He followed through on the suggestion. To his surprise, he received consistent responses about his best attributes: well-honed listening skills, an ability to ask insightful and provocative questions, a natural gift for reframing, and a calming presence.

One friend summarized the list of skills by saying, "Basically, you are a group facilitator." The suggestion was so specific that he ran with it. Luckily, there were many opportunities to be a facilitator in the Bay Area's progressive culture. He could help groups have difficult conversations, address how to work more effectively as a team, or discuss strategies for enacting social change initiatives. He experienced firsthand the energetic boost of having his intrinsic purpose align with the needs of others.

Freely Functioning

The discussion of calling implies self-identity. In Robert Kegan's developmental model, we see how calling helps us to individuate from highly socialized belonging to become more autonomous, self-responsible, and uniquely fulfilled. His description of the fifth order of development is referred to as self-transforming and, as we said previously, is marked by the ability to take multiple perspectives, engage with complexity, and relinquish or update notions of self. The self-transforming mind consistently invites changes in perspective, ideas, and identity. This mind cultivates a presence and mindfulness, allowing full engagement in the present moment without the constraint of preconceived ideas about who we are or who we should be. Freedom from attachment to self-identity reduces resistance to what the moment offers and, in turn, curiosity about what we can learn.

Zenju Earthlyn Manuel Roshi wrote a beautiful personal essay entitled "Sweeping My Heart" that captures presence's redemptive and liberatory power.[3] She speaks about her experiences as a Black practitioner in her early days as a Zen student. She says,

> For me, a dark-skinned person of African descent, cleaning the temple as Zen practice felt inappropriate and uncomfortable when I was at the beginning of my training. When you are an older Black woman and a young White man tells you how to mop the floor during the work period, the experience is akin to being a maid or a reminder of slavery. Ordinary temple work is the kind of labor often relegated in this country to folks of color and poor people. It is work that can ensure a lower rank in society.

In her story, Zenju Roshi describes a decisive shift from a societal role rooted in identity and history to a function derived from presence, free from identity. Zenju Roshi now says that when she is sweeping, she knows that cleaning "is the motion arising from sitting meditation, not history repeating itself."⁴ She concludes that the ultimate reparation is true freedom from the poison of our oppression.

Having purpose frees us to contribute in consistent and beneficial ways. But cultivating presence can free us to engage with each moment more freely. We can engage wholeheartedly with life's challenges and opportunities, paying particular attention to the natural order of things, embracing spontaneity even as we develop patience, and contributing to harmony around us. With the distinction between self and others seen through, we rely far less on our dualistic thinking to address our predicaments and dilemmas, allowing the greater movements to unfold. We cease to be so afraid, moving in the world with relaxation and confidence.

Freed from the demands of self-identity, there is no pressure to be good, perform, or do something else. When I am facilitating a group, I am facilitating. When I am playing with a baby, I am playing with the baby. When I am sweeping the zendo, I am sweeping the zendo. There is no sense of the right and wrong, good and bad, for and against mentality. We simply make adjustments and flow, like a basketball player who receives a pass, jumps, and shoots without the thought of the earlier missed shot. There is no preoccupation with outcomes, no concern about what will look good or whether others will approve. In other words, we function freely without self-orientation, fully present and engaged in undivided activity.

Gabe became a seeker at a young age. The aspiration to awaken, to penetrate the great matter of life and death completely occupied his attention, and he minimized other pursuits such as career building, experiencing them to be hollow and meaningless. Intrinsic and extrinsic purposes were not synergizing. At that point, he says that he related to his nine-to-five job as a means to keep a roof over his head, put food on the table, and provide enough money to travel and attend meditation retreats. He just could not see a way to bring his work and practice together.

He recalls that this dichotomy began to shift when he attended his first Zen retreat with me at Two Arrows. It started like any Zen retreat would: with silence, sitting, work practice, meals, a dharma talk each day, and then, of course, more sitting. However, a few days in, during the middle of a sitting period, I broke the silence and said to the group, "There is a conflict among some of you that has been in the background, but it is starting to affect the container we have created for meditation. So, let's address it. Please rearrange the room in two concentric circles."

Gabe tells me he was surprised and confused about what was going on. He had never participated in a meditation retreat where we interrupted the schedule for anything, let alone to bring a conflict into the open. This would be the first time he saw me facilitate.

The group having the conflict was on the staff and helping to run the retreat. I helped them communicate and navigate their tensions and disagreements. Gabe was surprised that I could be relatively calm throughout the whole exchange, which was quite hot. By the end of the conversation, we were able to clarify the conflict and forge new agreements about working together that all of us could participate in.

Then, just as quickly as we entered the conflict, we reset the room for zazen and returned to sitting. Gabe recounts that he felt a palpable difference in the quality of our energy. The surfacing of the conflict and its resolution increased our vitality and led to deeper coherence in our group. He remembers how the coherence infused his sitting, which was stronger and more stable than before. The new agreements contributed to making the container for our practice more powerful.

I don't shy away from bringing difficulties out into the group because waking up is not a private endeavor but belongs to us all. Everyone has strengths and weaknesses; everyone has insights and blind spots. We are stronger together, and we can learn to genuinely support one another's practice and develop our relationship skills. Conflict is nothing to be ashamed of. Rather, it is an opportunity to experience the unity that underlies the division and learn how to use the energy creatively.

Later, Gabe asked me, "Where did you learn to do THAT?"

"I work as a mediator and a facilitator," I responded.

Gabe recounts that he wasn't expecting it to be that straightforward. For the first time, he saw his intention to awaken and his work in the world as one thing. Instead of his aspiration to wake up overshadowing and downgrading all other pursuits, he saw that they were all the same thing. His practice is his life. Now, he says that he doesn't distinguish Zen training from his facilitation work. It is all one call, one great function.

He committed to Zen practice after that retreat. Then, he spent several summers in Torrey sitting zazen, maintaining the property, and taking in the natural world. He learned to sit alone and found company in the Buddha ancestors and support in the ritual forms. He also joined in facilitator training with me and continued developing his interpersonal skills. Now, he could see the practice of sitting still and aware positively informing his facilitation work. His presence became more clarified, and his skills evolved and became practicable. He learned to perceive the inherent wholeness of groups, using it to bring them to agreement.

Committing to practice in which our uniqueness serves the needs of others is the fulfillment of our calling. Cultivating presence empties us of anything that separates us from this moment, allowing us to meet it fully and wholeheartedly. As Maezumi Roshi extolls, "The best way to realize our wholeness is to do zazen and practice Buddhadharma as one's own life." As unique individuals, we may be ourselves, functioning freely and fully, in service to each other and life itself.

6

INSPIRED TO WAKE UP

Diane Musho Hamilton

All sentient beings are essentially Buddhas.
—Zen Master Hakuin

I once asked a friend to tell me the story of how she first began a spiritual practice. She described how she was sitting quietly at the table one day and was suddenly encompassed by the most exquisite experience of love. It was so powerful, she said, that she sat there for several hours. After that, she was compelled to seek the source of that astonishing feeling and learn how to access it anytime. Eventually, she discovered a nondual school of Hinduism and has remained a loyal practitioner of that path since.

I have another friend who describes how she was going about a typical day in Los Angeles driving on the freeway when suddenly it occurred to her that she didn't know who she was. She literally did not know. She became consumed by the question, earnestly and persistently asking, "Who am I?" After several years of inquiry, she found her identity in a Christian contemplative tradition.

My husband, Michael Zimmerman, came to Zen after his wife died of cancer at forty-two. He naturally searched for solace in his grief while he served as the chief justice of the Utah Supreme Court and was the sole parent of his three young daughters. One evening, he decided to attend an introduction to Zen class at the local Zen Center, along with two students from the nearby university. A Polish woman taught the class, and without so much as an opening icebreaker or warm hello, she began by saying flatly,

"In Buddhism, there is no hope."

Michael, who intimately knew the disappointment of hope and devastation of loss, felt a flood of relief hearing her words. The following week, he returned full of energy to meditate, while the other two students never returned.

Entering the Way

In the Zen tradition, the terms *awakening* or *waking up* refer to a fundamental shift in perspective. It indicates liberation from suffering of our separate sense of self and awakening to our interconnectedness and inherent well-being. When the persistent wants and needs of the ego abate, clarity and compassion result, and we are freed from chronic dissatisfaction. The practice for realizing this is zazen, or sitting meditation, and people come to the practice in various ways.

Over the years, I have heard many stories about how people have come to our Zen Center. Many find our center on the internet or join a free online talk as an introduction. Sometimes people describe hearing about our practice through a friend or being persuaded by a lover to come along and join a sitting period. Some arrive after reading a book or jumping feet first into a longer meditation retreat or sesshin. Occasionally, someone experiences an uncanny coincidence or synchronicity that prompts them to meditate. I was told once about a dream that prompted one woman to seek out Zen. Several people have recounted that they made the leap after a night of hard drinking and decided to find another way to live their lives.

A student told me how he found the Two Arrows Zen Center on the web and then drove over a few streets to our building. The first time, he said, he circled the block, scouted out the building, and then drove immediately back home. The second time he pulled into the parking lot, sat for a while in his car, then turned around and went home again. On the third trip over, he finally got the courage to enter the building, and nobody was there when he did. Not a soul. He left immediately, and it took him some months to gather the courage to come back again.

People have lots of reasons to try meditation. They are looking for stress reduction or a method for calming their minds and nervous systems. Sometimes they come for company, community, spiritual guidance, or new exploration. They have an intuition that sitting meditation might be good for them; perhaps it will bring clarity, meaning, or purpose to their lives. It might even help them cultivate their creativity or fulfill their dreams. Finally, and most importantly, seekers arrive wanting to become enlightened. In other words, they long to be freed from the grip of self-identity and the pressure to constantly try to fulfill the wants and needs of the ego.

Other people suffer from a sense of foreboding and wonder how to cope. They see climate chaos disrupting life around the world and are acutely aware of other looming crises. They are disturbed by the widening disparity between rich and poor, the renewed threat of nuclear war, and the pressures from increasing polarization that they fear is imperiling our social stability. Some of them talk about their worry over the advancement of artificial general intelligence (AGI), and they wonder how to face an uncertain, anxiety-ridden future.

The Buddha emphasized that impermanence is a fact of our life and uncertainty is a fixture of the human experience. He acknowledged that pain is inherent in existence, but additional layers of suffering can be overcome. He provided instructions for how to work with our own mind and heart, to see reality clearly, and to respond to our world intelligently, effectively, and compassionately.

His approach requires committed engagement and lots of practice, but arguably, investing in spiritual practice is the best way to prepare for uncertainty and change. His advice is to come to terms with the implacable truths of existence; cultivate mindfulness and awareness;

and learn to live neither asleep, nor overwhelmed, nor terribly afraid. It doesn't mean we never experience difficult mind states. But it does mean that we can receive and release them because we recognize them as states that come and go. All the while, our familiarity with ever-present awareness builds.

I came to practice after a series of encounters with death. Seven good friends died within four months of each other, from February to June of my junior year in high school. I was confronted by mortality and questioned how to be human given the fact we die. I was intuitively drawn to meditation as a response to my questions about life and death and the sorrow that came with my losses.

The very first time I sat with a group, I had a strong experience. Sustaining attention for several hours in the here, I felt myself relax. My mind soon quieted down from preoccupation with my thoughts, and I felt strangely fulfilled. Without explanation, I found this presence and relaxation put my heart at ease. The world suddenly appeared friendlier, and my challenges seemed workable. This engendered a deep curiosity in me about the power of meditation, and one experience formed the basis for the years of practice to follow.

I feel lucky to have come upon a spiritual tradition that finally scratched the existential itch. The Buddhist lineage has been the road map for my spiritual journey, including practice instructions, teachings, and insights that have helped me. I have had excellent teachers who brought the teachings to life.

Zen isn't for everybody. For many people, the idea of practicing Zen would be similar to entering a monastery in the Middle Ages, with black robes, shaved heads, chanting in low tones, and a rigorous sitting schedule that begins before dawn. It feels like it is from another time and another place. And it is. But it also isn't. The Buddhist tradition excels at putting on the accouterments of an era or place, and like all things, it evolves over time. Whether robes, suits, or yoga pants, the outfits simply dress up our timeless nature. The teachings and instructions are perennial. This is what makes this practice so dependable. One doesn't have to become a full-fledged Buddhist to benefit from the teachings and practice, but cultivating a daily meditation routine goes a long way in quieting our minds and soothing our hearts.

Inspired to Practice

How do people become inspired, or even more importantly, stay inspired to practice? Where does the energy come from that sparks the interest and fuels an ongoing commitment? There are as many different forms of inspiration as there are people in our Zen practice and sangha. We each engage in the same practice of zazen, study the precepts together, and deepen our bonds with friends in the dharma. But each of us must learn to follow our own heart and listen to our unique bubbling of inspiration.

There are many ways I receive inspiration to practice. A lot of it comes from watching others. The example of those friends and students with natural devotion touches me. They bring commitment, heart, compassion, and sensitivity to relationships in the practice. They are the ones who build sanghas and create community. They engender appreciation for the people who share their deepest questions. They value the intimacy of sitting together in the same silence, sharing a powerful, implicit intention. I have heard people talk about the feeling of support that comes from practicing with others. They describe how a moment of struggle during zazen is dispelled when glancing across the zendo and seeing someone sitting strong. Or how a moment of unexpected kindness can alleviate a sore heart or vanquish fatigue. I have heard people remark on the relief they feel from the pressure of always having to be a stand-out individual and how relieving it is to be part of a practice community.

Other people are thrilled with dharma study, and thoroughly enjoy reading books, commentary, and scholarship. They love the vast library of the Buddhist tradition and how it expresses its meanings, preserves and evolves its elegant ideas, and offers poetic expressions of truth. Some people participate in practice through artistic engagement in Zen, which promotes the fine relationship to detail, including calligraphy, flower arranging, and precise enactments of ceremony. These are lovers of beauty, collaborating with reality to open our senses and excite creativity.

Some people move me with their work ethic and love of physical challenges. They get energy from getting up early, putting up and taking down tents, trimming trees, dragging hoses around the property, and beautifying the garden. When a repair needs to be made, they gladly do it. They are at home with the equipment in the shed and enjoy sharpening tools and arranging extension cords. They are willing to paint, put up, and take down fences, and like nothing more than a trip to the building supply store or the local greenhouse. For them, physical engagement is the complete expression of dharma, and everyone benefits from their work, especially the plants.

I have a lot of respect for the people who practice as couples. Seriously. I'm impressed with how they treat each other, talk to each other, and offer support, taking turns with the schedule and with their children. Ours is definitely not an old-school monastery, so it requires innovation. There is a committed group of parents who are brave enough to bring their whole families to retreat. These young families figure out how to alternate the sitting periods, trade off childcare, and support each other throughout the weeks in retreat. Being around people who cultivate genuinely collaborative relationships and negotiate in good faith is a privilege.

Finally, our kitchen is managed by Julia, a trained chef whose food is genuinely inspired. Her menus are healthy, varied, and balanced, with a deep understanding of seasoning and the complementary nature of flavors and textures. The particulars of her palette combine to create tremendous unity in the overall meal. She creates a kitchen full of practitioners who work well together while washing, chopping, and frying. In preparing food, they understand coherence in tasting and moving as one. At our retreats, we eat well, enjoy the satisfaction of good food, and wash our bowls after every meal. I sometimes joke that if you have a strong will to power in our tiny Zen school, the most coveted promotion is to the rank of the dishwashing supervisor.

Boundless Aspiration

I have always been deeply inspired by the words of Dogen Zenji when I was first introduced to his writing by my teacher. Eihei Dogen was a Japanese Zen master who lived from 1200 to 1253 and founded the Soto School of Zen in Japan. He is known for his profound, poetic writing, which elucidates the inextricability of enlightenment and ordinary life. Zazen, or sitting meditation, is its method.

Dogen writes that the inspiration (or aspiration, depending on the translation) to awaken is evidence of our enlightened nature. In one of his essays, entitled "Thusness," he quotes another master, Yunju, who says, "You are trying to attain thusness, yet you are already a person of thusness." Dogen explains thusness to mean "immediately getting to unsurpassable enlightenment." He says, "Because of thusness, you arouse a boundless aspiration for enlightenment. Once this aspiration arises, you let go of what you have been *playing with*."

Letting go of what you have been playing with could be philosophy, literature, or psychology if it is not helping. It means giving up whatever preoccupies your mind, burdens your heart, or interferes with the direct experience of your senses. It involves relinquishing notions that create the persistent feeling that you are not enough or interrupting the voice that says you must be more, want more, and get more.

Because Dogen Zenji says clearly,

How do you know you are a person of thusness?
You know it because you want to attain thusness.[1]

He goes on, saying that in letting go of what you have been playing with, you come forward to hear what you have never heard and realize what is not yet realized.

In other words, you are inspired to study and to practice further, which has been true for me. He makes the point that this inspiration is not apart from you. It is not an effort or accomplishment of the personal self. It is self-arising, from this very body and mind because this very life is one of thusness.

Dogen says this boundless aspiration is evidence that this body-mind is selfless in all the world of the ten directions. How do you know that such is the case? He says, "You know it because your body and mind are not you; they appear in the entire world of the ten directions."[2]

People often struggle with the notion of selflessness. This insight can seem threatening to our preoccupation with self-identity, but it comes easily and naturally when you allow it. When we walk in the landscape, our eyes catch the beauty of the light, and our attention finds the setting sun on the horizon line. We take in the immensity without self-identity. A bristlecone pine lives on for hundreds, even thousands, of years. While each of us comes and goes, life goes on with the bristlecone. The life of the forest, the time frames of the great red cliffs, and the boundlessness of the space at night bedazzled with stars are the self, according to Master Dogen.

Dogen Zenji goes on to say because we are selfless, we can manifest our body and mind as the ten directions, and the ten directions are the illumination of oneself.

How to be this selfless?

You are already such a person.

Yunju says, "You are trying to attain thusness, yet you are already a person of thusness. As you are already a person of thusness, why be worried about thusness?"[3]

I wish I had known that in college. I could have used a spiritual friend to assure me that my regret, dread, and anxiety, while painful, were also thusness. Often, it isn't raw inspiration that brings us to practice. We are, instead, simply looking for a way to suffer less. Both Gabe and I were college students who were in a deep existential crisis. Somehow, we both discovered the Buddhist tradition and were inspired to study. The feelings of angst and dread we suffered were the flip side of the excitement that comes from inspiration, and exactly what brought us to the practice. It is counterintuitive to see how intrinsic they are to the path. Rumi says,

If God said, Pay homage
to everything that has brought me into your life.
There would not be one thought,
one feeling, or one experience that
I would not bow to.

So, whether we prefer it or don't prefer it, whether it gives us joy or causes us pain, whether we are being cheered on by others or unfairly maligned, somehow there is room for all of it, and everything is in its place. This life is thusness. We are reminded to appreciate our lives even when scared or threatened. We remember to laugh out loud at our bouts of foolishness or anger.

Through practice, we can free ourselves so that goodwill is recognized as innate to us. Our freedom includes responding to life, contributing, and offering our unique talents and energy. Recognizing that we are fundamentally intact, nothing is lost through letting go. Letting go again and again lightens our life and expands our perspective. We take in more. We come to peace with life's difficulties and feel connected to our innate awakened heart. We practice, we realize, and we let it go again. We experience the power of inspiration, remembering we all seek the same thing: to be a full, complete human being.

7

PRACTICE IS ENLIGHTENMENT

Gabriel Kaigen Wilson

I have failed Zen practice many times, but Zen practice has never failed me. —Diane Musho Hamilton

What does it mean to turn our attention to that which is reliable under all circumstances? To cultivate an awareness beyond our concepts and ideas so that we can access the sensation of well-being no matter what happens in our lives or the world? What would it mean to trust our existence is inherently worthy despite the fact we will die? We must be willing to look beyond the shiny objects that capture, fascinate, and exhaust us to something deeper and more durable. To discover this, we need reliable instructions, guidance, and practice. There are many old adages about the importance of practice in life. "Practice makes perfect," or as they say in golf circles, "The more I practice, the luckier I get."

Anytime we engage our body and mind, repeating a pattern over and over, we are practicing. If we devote ourselves to cooking, we practice in the kitchen with food, flavors, heat, culinary techniques, and tools. As artists, we practice with form—lines, textures, colors, patterns, and light. If we are athletes, we practice with the body, with will, strength, timing, and precision. And if we are meditators, we practice sitting still with our whole body and mind.

Simple rituals like brushing our teeth or doing the laundry are daily practices. They offer consistent opportunities for mindfully taking care of things. Ordinary tasks like these contribute to our lives' rhythm, quality, and groundedness. In the same way, practices designed to sharpen our expertise or deepen our artistry give our existence depth and beauty. Meditation is a practice that cultivates the subtle substratum of our lives so that we experience continuity through time, equanimity with the ups and downs, and a persistent sense of well-being, even when life circumstances become difficult or uncertain.

Anything that we repeat over and over is a practice. Our practices are not always positive, nor are they necessarily conscious. We might practice anger, consistently becoming offended or mad that the world isn't how we want it to be. We could constantly worry over our politics and not realize the habit of complaint we have formed. We may have gotten used to shopping online because, in the short term, it seems to relieve anxiety until the packages pile up on the doorstep or remain unopened in the closet, creating more angst. Some habits are even more destructive, like using drugs for fun until that drug habit is no longer a choice but an addiction.

For better or worse, by repeating something again and again, we create a deep, habitual groove in the body-mind, and momentum builds from the repetition. We practice many different things, whether or not the practices are good for us. So, we have to learn to make conscious choices about what we are going to practice, why it is important, and how best to cultivate the particular discipline. Over time, we benefit from our intention, the practice, and its fruition.

Zen Practice

Zazen is called the authentic gate to Zen practice. Zazen is simply seated meditation. In our tradition, posture is key because a strong, stable, and relaxed posture supports a clarified, open mind. We sit cross-legged with a firm seat, elevated spine, relaxed shoulders and jaw, a soft face and gaze. The heart center is open, and the hands form a circle in our lap, thumbs touching. This gesture is called the cosmic mudra, representing wholeness and continuity. The posture is balanced and elegant, and one can feel the dependability of the form by simply looking at it. It is best described by the word *dignified* because to sustain this posture, we must be centered.

As in all sitting meditation, attention to the breath is essential. The breath is lighter than the body but denser than the mind. Focusing on the breath in the here and now harmonizes body and mind. It can be used as the focus for mindfulness, to develop concentration, or to relax the body and settle the mind at the outset of the meditation practice. Focus on the breath immediately calms the body and reminds us to lighten up.

The breath provides a fundamental reference point for the mind because it is always present until the moment of death. When the mind is agitated or chaotic, we can focus lightly on the inhalation and exhalation at the tip of the nose, experiencing the coolness of the breath on the inhale and the warmth of the breath on the exhale. As Lama Surya Das reminds us, "With every breath, the old moment is lost, and a new moment arrives."[1] With our attention on breathing, he says we live in harmony with the rhythm of the universe, letting go of the person we used to be.

When the body and breath are harmonized, we focus on the mind. Initially, the mind is considered to be the activity of cognition: thoughts, images, memories, and internal dialogue flowing through our awareness, like the experience of scrolling through a smartphone. This flow of activity lacks continuity or logic, yet we are compelled to pay attention as though meaning and value are somewhere in there if only we keep the scroll going.

But we discover quite quickly how incoherent our mind stream is. Mental content is often fragmented and speedy, and our thinking is oppositional: yes, then no; good, then bad; for, then against. The speed of mind and the seesawing of thought create tension in our nervous system and stress hormones in the body. So, when we sit down to be still, the body may have come to rest, but the mind is not quiet. This agitation initially makes sitting practice difficult because it can be unpleasant. The body may also feel uncomfortable, with neck and shoulders sore from carrying tension or knees that are inflexible and hurting.

But in time and with practice, we adapt. We become accustomed to gently establishing the posture, and the body becomes relaxed and stronger. We learn to breathe naturally, rhythmically, with our whole body allowing the mind to settle easily. We cease trying to control our thoughts and emotions but allow them to come and go in the open space of mind, and we come to see how the Mind, with a capital *M*, is far greater than our thoughts, feelings, memories, and self-identity. We will explore the actual practice of "just sitting" in chapter 8. However, I want to share the benefits I have experienced after establishing the practice of zazen.

As soon as I started sitting regularly, I noticed a subtle improvement in my mood and my outlook. I began to feel the well-being of letting go of identification with the barrage of thoughts and feelings, connecting more fully to the present moment with all of my senses. I learned to allow whatever arose during sitting—thoughts, feelings, or sensations in the body—to have its place. I also found I could include pain rather than running from it. Eventually, I learned to surrender the focus on the objects of meditation, such as body sensations and mental activity, and developed a taste for identification with awareness. Awareness is analogized to the sky; in that wide-open space, there is room for all experiences to arise. They come and go like a thunderstorm moves over the mountain in the summertime and then clears out, revealing an utterly boundless sky.

In time, the practice transformed my relationship with myself and the world. I became lighter, less self-concerned, and more acutely aware that I was sometimes free of self-identity entirely. Paradoxically, I became much more at home in my own skin. I also recognized the world as it is and that it isn't designed to please or accommodate my preferences. But I can make a positive contribution to it, cultivating care and compassionate activity in response to its many challenges. As I continued to sit and study Buddhadharma, the practice imprinted itself as a permanent, invaluable feature of my life.

Styles of Practice

Some people can practice sitting on their own. There are many stories of monks living alone in the mountains or yogis practicing for years in caves by themselves. Roshi's practice is dynamic and changeable and expresses itself in her solo practice. She doesn't have routines. But she describes how the practice just happens in her life, especially when she is alone, walking in the foothills or in the desert in Utah. Often she likes to walk in the nearby city cemetery, famous for being the largest municipal cemetery in the United States. It is big with many winding roads, rock walls, memorials, religious statues, and headstones. There is a lot of grass and trees, so a suitable spot—there are so many—appears, and she sits down there for a while. She appreciates being free of wanting or needing anything other than to sit still. Sometimes she sits at home alone in her room on her meditation cushion; other times she sits on the living room couch or outside on the porch. She says she likes the ease of this, the informality, and the spontaneity. Sometimes she sits longer, sometimes shorter, and sometimes meditates while lying in the tub because it feels nice.

My wife Alana and I practice together. We are committed to Zen, and it shapes our priorities and the flow of our calendar. Our shared practice is like the sun's gravity that brings coherency and meaning to our family system. We organize our days so that practice is a central feature. We take turns preparing dinner, going to the Zen Center, and caring for the baby, for example. Often, Alana comes back from sitting with shining eyes and a warmth that nourishes our whole family. The night out with sangha sweeps away the stir-craziness that may have built up in me. The other powerful effect of partnership in practice is that it creates natural pauses when we get wrapped up in the momentum of daily life. My grandmother says, "Love is not only looking into your beloved's eyes but looking with each other in the same direction."

There is practicing solo, practicing in partnership, and practicing with a group. When sitting together in person, zazen takes place in the zendo, or meditation hall. The zendo is simple and unadorned except for the altar that provides a focal point for meditation and ceremonies. Usually, a figure—the Bodhisattva of Wisdom—sits in zazen on the altar, along with flowers, candles, and incense. The light is low, the room silent, and the atmosphere is pristine and dense with stillness.

People often remark on how beautiful our zendo is. They refer to a sense of beauty, stillness, and shared intention. You can feel those qualities even when it is empty. But a zendo filled with people sitting together is potent, as individuals draw on the energy of the group to support their own zazen.

For most of us, sitting for longer periods in a group is easier than sitting alone. It is inspiring to get up early together to sit at dawn or to watch the light in the zendo change as the sun sets, the room becoming dark as night falls all around. There is an unspoken sense of belonging, connection, and mutual support as we practice to accomplish the Buddha Way together.

Sitting in silence together or performing ceremonies, the unity of group activity is rich, even magical at times. Whether bowing together, chanting, or lighting incense, these rituals help us to deepen our social bonds, create shared meaning, and participate in beauty. Ritual is highly conformist because we all do the same things at the same time. But it provides a context for letting go. Rather than asserting our individuality, we surrender to the choreography, rhythms, and energy. We become one body and one voice as we enact different symbolic gestures, using drums, gongs, and bells to highlight and convey our shared intentions as we chant the lines of sacred texts. They transport us into a boundless and timeless domain.

Deeply the Same, Utterly Unique

I have accepted Ken Wilber's view that the ways we are taught to practice in most religious traditions arise from a socialized level of human development in which the imperatives of belonging, conformity, rule following, and submitting oneself to authority are primary.[2] The traditional values of duty, obedience, loyalty, and self-sacrifice are central to this worldview, especially in religious traditions.

This traditional bent can turn people away from formal practice because traditional values don't reflect other waves of human development that we have grown accustomed to in North America—for example, the modern emphasis on our individuality and the ability to achieve, or the postmodern interest in our subjective opinions, feelings, sensitivity, and various personal and cultural identities.

In our Two Arrows Zen practice, we attempt to include multiple value sets and recognize our practitioners' unique expressions because, like the universal, the highly particular is the other essential feature of reality. Each practitioner is very unique in how they practice. Where Musho Roshi's practice is dynamic like the wind, the practice of her husband, Michael Zimmerman, is like a stable mountain.

Musho Roshi often remarks about how she admires her husband, Michael Mugaku Zimmerman, and his relationship with zazen. He sits according to routine, strong and unobstructed, like it was the most natural thing in the world. Even though he started sitting at the age of fifty, thirty years later he sits with a rare composure and commitment. He never uses the word *passion* to describe his practice, but he is energized, straightforward, and unencumbered in his approach to practice. He has never once complained about the challenges of sitting, and he just keeps doing it.

As we said in the previous chapter, some people in our practice have deeply devotional hearts. They bring tremendous care and compassion to the practice and to others. Some people are thrilled with the study of dharma, its elegant concepts and its unique expression of truth. Some people flourish with physical work, while others love the company of the community or the intimacy with the teacher. But everyone in our practice community opens to the space of Mind during zazen including the stillness, the silence, and the vastness of the red canyons and cliffs where we practice in Southern Utah.

The trick in any community is to honor our differences but to recognize that we are inherently the same. As Dogen Zenji reminds us, Buddha Nature is abundant in each of us, and when we recognize this, all things belong and are experienced in their natural place. Master Dogen tells us that "this profound reality is not actualized without practice, and it is not experienced without realization."[3] So, we practice to realize this for ourselves, to experience our interconnectedness firsthand, and to act with compassion and kindness toward all things. Through practice, we relinquish the belief in our separateness and in a real way, discover the greater whole to which we belong.

8

JUST SITTING

Diane Musho Hamilton

The true Dharma correctly transmitted by Buddha ancestors
is just sitting. —Dogen Zenji

When I was a baby, not yet a year old, I started to walk. My mom
described how I had begun pulling myself upright at the coffee table or couch, taking toddler steps around it. Then she said, "I noticed
that suddenly you had stopped walking and were just sitting." She
took me to the doctor and discovered that my red blood cell count
was extremely depleted. They couldn't locate a source for my anemia,
but after a blood transfusion, I resumed pulling myself up and began
walking again.

Whenever my mother told this story, and she told it many times
over the years, the phrase "just sitting" stood out in my mind. When I
began practicing Zen many years later, I heard this expression again.
The Japanese word *shikantaza* translates simply as "just sitting," and
it is the practice at the heart of our Zen school.

The word *zazen* refers to Zen meditation practiced in the sitting
position. From the outside, it looks the same: Everyone sits cross-
legged and upright, hands joined resting in their lap, eyes cast to the
floor in a soft gaze, and everything is silent. However, there may be

variations in what the practitioner does with their attention inside. One may be counting breaths, while another explores an emotional state, and a third penetrates a life question. But when one practices shikantaza, there is upright sitting and breathing, but there is no specific object of contemplation other than panoramic awareness itself.

The Soto Zen teacher and scholar Taigen Dan Leighton describes shikantaza as objectless meditation that "focuses on clear, nonjudgmental, panoramic attention to all the myriad arising phenomena in the present experience." He says, "This just sitting is a verb rather than a noun, the dynamic activity of being fully present."[1] Shikantaza allows all things to be experienced as they are, including awareness itself. Zen Master Dogen referred to shikantaza as the "upright gate of ease and joy."[2] The practice is not about achieving a special state of mind; instead, it involves surrendering ideas about spiritual practice and being present to everything as it is. In this immediacy and simplicity, we can contact the ease and joy Dogen Zenji is talking about, experiencing freedom, calm, and fulfillment.

Taming the Horse, Riding the Mind

I came to Buddhadharma when I was twenty-three-years old. I had been studying literature and philosophy, but I needed to make a living, so I applied to several master's programs in psychology instead. I had heard of Naropa Institute and thought that a program emphasizing direct experience would interest me. I distinctly remember the day I received the program materials in the mail. Two things stood out to me. One was the elegance of the Tibetan Buddhist graphics on a rich, purple background, which I loved. The second was the title of an article by Chöygam Trungpa, Rinpoche, entitled "Taming the Horse, Riding the Mind."

I grew up riding horses, and my early meditation experience began naturally when I rode in the mountains on summer days as a kid. At the heart of riding are a stable seat and an upright spine. One learns to relax and attend to one's mind and body, as well as that of the animal. The training in attention is good for both of us.

I remember how taking a long ride on horseback allowed me time to think and become acquainted with my mind. I could watch my thoughts, mulling things over, until they gradually quieted down, and there was nothing left to think about. I recall a particular sensation of presence, vividness, and simplicity after a day in the mountains. On the way home, my mind had emptied, my senses opened up, and I noticed changes in the weather, the sound of the horse's hooves clipping along, the occasional bird taking flight, or a cat crouching on a front porch. I remember the weight and balance of my body in rhythm with the horse's movements, its head and strong, curved neck bobbing toward home. It was all deeply satisfying.

The title of Trungpa Rinpoche's article provoked the muscle memory of a whole-bodied ability to be present with my body and mind connected to the environment. I felt instantly excited. I applied, and within a few months I had begun to develop what became a lifelong sitting practice.

Effort and Effortlessness

From the outside, Zen practice can seem daunting. It involves rigorous schedules, precise forms, and unwavering demands on your attention, especially when training with a teacher in a residential setting. It requires a willingness to push oneself, whether early in the morning when the alarm sounds or at the end of a long day when skipping an evening sitting period is tempting.

Everyone encounters discomfort, physical pain, or fatigue when practicing for extended periods, but we discover how to stay present and endure. We contend with many stuck emotional patterns but eventually give up our defensiveness. We face mental hurdles such as boredom or doubt, even after years of practice, and learn to keep going. We become softer, even as we get tougher. I appreciate the demands that Zen training makes because, without its requirements, I would be a casualty of my own love of comfort. I appreciate the friends in the practice because they also like challenges.

However, when we come to the cushion and settle into sitting still, we give up pushing. The reversal is counterintuitive, in contrast to our habit of perpetually striving for more, better, and different; shikantaza unwinds that tendency. Instead, we sit still, acknowledging objects of awareness such as sensations, feelings, thoughts, sounds, movements, et cetera, while relinquishing our preferences and fixed agendas. We allow impressions to come and go naturally. The body continues to be relaxed and upright. The breath occurs in its natural rhythm, and the mind remains open, accommodating changes in perceptions without regard for our judgments of for or against.

Most importantly, we sustain attention on that which doesn't change: the open field of awareness itself. By being fully present, we glimpse boundlessness, timelessness, that which is unconditioned and all-pervasive. Over time, we enter the "upright gate of ease and joy." Genuine appreciation for our life and compassion for all things blossom naturally in this open, formless field. One ancient Chinese master, known for the depth of his realization and his evocative writing, says this:

> The matter of oneness cannot be learned at all.
> The essence is to empty,
> And to open out body and mind,
> as expansive as the great emptiness of space.
> Naturally in the entire territory all is satisfied.[3]

There is a common misunderstanding that sitting still equals passivity and disengagement from the world. The practice is dynamic in much the same way active listening skills impact a person who is speaking when they have the sudden sensation of being heard. Through stable, spacious sitting, our thinking calms down, our motives clarify, and wisdom appears timely, holistic, and relevant. Strangely, shikantaza makes us more functional. The mind clarifies through a quiet distillation process, and our activity refines. We see more vividly, feel more energy, and act with a singularity of purpose.

My life is not that of a patched-robe monk. I am a lay Zen practitioner who works as a mediator. I joke that I am a talented mediator with little training and a well-trained meditator with almost no natural talent. But they are essentially the same thing. Sitting meditation harmonizes the practitioner's body, breath, and mind, becoming one with the environment. In mediation, parties arrive with conflicts, differences, and emotional stress. The mediator brings them together, where they discover shared values and overlapping interests. They drop their unhelpful attachments, forging a working agreement that settles substantive issues, such as money, tasks, and time commitments, and a strategy for fulfilling their agreement. They come into harmony.

In other words, through the practice of mediation and meditation, two become one. Or even better, differences resolve by revealing preexisting, underlying commonalities. The sameness is evident in a conflict because people are so involved with one another and usually agree they have a conflict. As Yogi Berra once said, "We agree differently." Neither meditation nor mediation would be useful without the fact that while we appear divided, we accord.

I approach mediation in much the same way I approach sitting meditation. I intend to be of help, but I have to be open, without a series of preconceived ideas about what I think should happen. I familiarize myself with the dispute, much like meditation familiarizes me with my own mind. I listen to the disputants, receiving their stories, concerns, and distress, like I experience my own stories and pain while sitting—without judging. I drop the striving and grasping, letting the process and people do the work.

I let go from moment to moment, remaining present, holding my opinions lightly as the parties talk through their differences. I support the parties in finding common ground and assist them in cultivating an agreement. But I have to do so without an attachment to the outcome. There isn't much use for thoughts of "me and mine" in the mediation process. Similarly, self-identity only creates tension in sitting meditation. I joke sometimes that there is nothing more hellish than meditating as a self, at least until you can see it is empty.

Simple, but Not Easy

One student commented that sitting is easy; "It is the 'just' part that is challenging," he said. It takes practice to let go of seeking and striving, of clinging and grasping in the mind. It takes time to slough off our relentless, self-oriented conditioning; big expectations for an extraordinary experience; or sense of virtue over being able to sit still. It takes time to discover the timeless.

Paying attention to some subtleties can help. We can soften our internal voice. When we listen carefully, this voice often sounds harsh, like a military commander barking, preparing us for a fight rather than instructions from a trusted, experienced friend. I invite my students to take note of the sound of that inner voice, paying attention to its quality. One doesn't need to be harsh because shikantaza is not about effort; there is no battle to be fought or war to be won. We practice sitting in an atmosphere of openness without a gaining idea, as Kodo Sawaki Roshi said. Relaxing the drivenness and attending to the wholeness of experience; eventually, that demanding voice quiets to a whisper and gives way to the sounds of all things.

I encourage students to reflect on times when they naturally drop off self-concern when they are not in the zendo. Some recall letting go as they sink into a warm tub. Some describe the calm and expansiveness of looking at the horizon line at dusk. Some notice timelessness while taking a long drive. Some shed self-identity while stroking the fur of a pet. Some feel no-self-no-other while quietly feeding a baby or laughing out loud with their lover. We spontaneously stop seeking or grasping on these occasions and are unselfconsciously present. This innate ability to experience life fully and to be satisfied is cultivated through sitting still but is neither created, nor earned, nor accomplished. The gate to ease and joy opens spontaneously in different ways, and noticing it outside formal practice supports this recognition while on the cushion.

Sometimes, as a method of exploring the field of awareness, I invite identifying with awareness itself rather than with the objects of awareness. We simply complete the sentence stem, "As awareness, I am _____ (fill in the blank)." For example, as awareness, I am open. As awareness, I am ever present. As awareness, I am utterly inclusive. As awareness, I cannot be grasped. As awareness, I am free of identity. As awareness, I am beyond concepts. And so on. This exercise is not the practice of shikantaza, which doesn't focus on distinctions or conceptualize experience. But placing our attention exclusively on one or the other strengthens our capacity to discern objects of mind and the boundless territory in which they arise.

I want students to glean that True Nature, or Buddha Nature, is not a state. It doesn't come and go. It is ever present. It is free of form but permeates all things. It is not an "it" but a "this." All of this. All and everything as it is. Discursive thoughts, perpetual desires, relentless fears, attachment to beliefs and identities, and for/against thinking are part of it. They are not inherently bad. But they are preoccupations that create division in the mind, like clouds blocking out the sun or bringing rain to the picnic. Because the sun is always there, we can experience the full light of our True Nature when the weather of our mental habits and preoccupations clear away.

Oneness of Practice and Enlightenment

Shikantaza is not a means to an end. Dogen Zenji says that we don't practice to attain enlightenment. We practice, he says, because practice is enlightenment:

> To practice the Way singleheartedly is, in itself, enlightenment. There is no gap between practice and enlightenment or zazen and daily life.[4]

This emphasis undercuts goal orientation; it cuts through dualistic thinking and puts us directly in touch with inherent wholeness and completeness. Moreover, it points out that our desire to sit still, our yearning to realize ourselves, and the energy to keep going are evidence of our enlightened nature. It is because we are already enlightened that we practice.

Some people worry that this approach to practice breeds complacency. They believe that if I am already whole and endowed with my original nature, what is the use of formal study, a relationship with a teacher, and engagement with sangha? Why not be happy just being me? That is an excellent question; in fact, it is a question central to this style of practice.

I can see how for some people, the assertion of the oneness of practice and enlightenment gives permission to live life without a commitment to a spiritual practice. But for me, it has had the exact opposite effect. It made it possible for me to continuously practice in this tradition for most of my life from my college years through adulthood and now into the youth of old age. It has been there through all the delight and pain of being human. It has never wavered, and there is nothing that it has been unwilling to experience. I say that I have failed my practice many times, but it has never failed me. Not because I have thought to myself, "I'm already enlightened"—I'm pretty sure I have never had that thought—but because I have been encouraged to just sit, and by doing it, I have consistently experienced the inherent joy of sitting and the freedom of an open mind.

It has given me full permission to "be me," but in a different way than the conventional sense. It becomes quite clear that the self we usually think of is limited, bound by notions of self and other, by unstable swings of the ego, the ups and downs of good and bad fortune: not getting what we want, getting what we don't want, or getting what we want. But as we relax the grip of self-orientation, "I" gently gives way, and what I consider to be "me" changes. Master Dogen says that True Nature is abundant in all of us, but it is not realized without practice. Committed to sitting, we will discover our original nature for ourselves. We must practice to experience it, while doing it is the expression of enlightenment itself.

I have another experience from childhood that sticks with me. There is a home movie of my sister and me when she was about two years old, and I was three. It is summertime, and we are playing on the slide. She is climbing up the front of the slide in her sunsuit, working hard at it, slipping down, and climbing up again. She is clearly enjoying every minute of the challenge because she does it over and over again while my dad films her. I am in the background of the scene, just sitting at the top of the slide, content and quiet, watching her, and looking around at the expanse. It must have taken some effort to get up to the top of the slide, but in the home movie, I am just sitting with the whole world without regret or a gaining idea. The time is now, the place is here, and everything is exactly as it is.

9

TRUE IDENTITY

Gabriel Kaigen Wilson

You are originally unlimited and perfect. —Ramana Maharshi

I entered the Zen lineage well before I knew I did. I was initiated one day in college when I was dribbling the ball up the basketball court. I had done this so many times before when, out of nowhere, my heart broke into a loud, irregular rhythm. Terror immediately rang through me, my vision narrowed, and I simply put down the ball and walked off the court while the confused voices of my teammates called after me. This was my first direct encounter with the possibility of death. I was only twenty years old, and in the months following, I would experience about fifteen more events that sent me to the hospital.

A heart arrhythmia is an irregular heartbeat that occurs when the electrical signals that coordinate the heart's beating don't work correctly. In my case, the error in signaling caused the heart to beat too fast and irregularly, and there was nothing I could do about it. After so many experiences like this, something else happened.

The heart arrhythmia pulled me out of sleep one night. Having grown more familiar with these episodes, I did something different. Rather than calling a friend to take me to the campus hospital for monitoring, I decided to walk there. Along the way, I passed by a beautiful forty-foot totem pole with a park bench near its base. I thought to myself, "I'm not going to the hospital. I'm going to sit on this park bench and wait this out." So, I sat down under the steadying presence of the totem pole and tuned in fully to my experience.

The body knows when the heart is in trouble, and it causes a fight-or-flight response. The stress hormones released into the bloodstream create acute anxiety and an impulse to act. But after so many of these episodes, I knew there was nowhere to go. Instead, I just let myself experience my extreme bodily and mental distress. Every so often, a pang of terror would trigger a thought like, "Maybe I should go to the hospital." "What if my heart goes sideways while I'm out here?" But instead of acting, I chose to sit through the terror.

Over the course of two hours of anxiety and dread, a silent, steady, and unperturbed dimension of myself became more evident. The nerve-racking heart irregularity persisted, and so did my anxiety and fear. Yet, I felt as if it wasn't happening to me. I was simply the witness to it all. I could sit quietly with all of it in a state that I later learned was called equanimity. Finally, my heart rhythm settled down and became normal under the stillness and silence of that totem pole. I knew that I had awakened to a dimension of myself that I had not consciously recognized before.

I proceeded to sit through several more arrhythmias like that, experiencing a mixture of anxiety and equanimity. At times, I would feel captured by the tremendous discomfort of the moment, and at other times, I would feel the profound silence and stillness. I wanted to learn to contact this stillness and equanimity more reliably—the same stillness and equanimity that Shakyamuni Buddha recognized 2,500 years before. As a young seeker, Shakyamuni Buddha left the comfort of his familiar world and entered the wilderness of the spiritual search. He had been born into wealth and status, but his privilege didn't satisfy him. He had observed quite clearly our human predicament. He saw that we are born not knowing where we come from or why we are here. He saw up close how we seek pleasure, comfort, and security, avoiding painful and uncertain situations. Despite our best efforts to maintain our comfort, we may become ill, experience misfortune, and eventually get old and die.

Under these circumstances, the Buddha wanted to discover a deeper, more abiding truth. He wanted his insight to inform him how best to live. He embarked on a spiritual approach of the time: extreme self-discipline and asceticism. But after years of intense fasting, yoga, and the denial of all indulgences, he decided to find a middle way. He committed to using his energies to penetrate his own mind and see into his conditioning. The depth of his inquiry revealed that we have a fundamental misunderstanding of the world and ourselves that gives rise to dissatisfaction.

Committed to sitting still and watching his mind, he saw that what we call a "self" or "I" is a combination of an ever-changing series of sensations, emotions, thoughts, interpretations, and reactions to our surroundings and circumstances. The Buddha said that these impressions combine to form the basis of our anxiety and reactivity and are the source of our suffering.[1] In other words, the idea we have of ourselves has no corresponding, stable reality, but we spend much of our time thinking about ourselves and our predicaments.

The act of self-identification automatically creates an experience of separation because I am here and everything else is there. It produces harmful thoughts of me and mine, desire and craving, aversion and hatred. He concluded that identification with "I" is the source of our most persistent human problems. At the same time, he said that anyone who sees suffering and dissatisfaction can also see the source of that suffering and how to relieve it. When we see this clearly, we can take steps on the path to relieve suffering for ourselves and others.[2]

A Separate Self

The Buddha's doctrine of no-self is a radical proposition, especially in a culture that prizes individual identity and independent achievement. In school, we are taught to form our own opinions, follow our passions, own our narrative, and develop our brand. The very idea that there is no substance to the self is incomprehensible. And yet, it is easy to observe in others; when they are free of self-consciousness, they are light, enjoyable, and available to connect. But when our friends and significant others are burdened with self-concern, they are heavy-hearted, unhappy, or agitated. And an inflated ego is always unpleasant and overbearing. That is not to say that we don't have real dilemmas in life or challenges related to our self-identity, but what if we just get a little bit curious about what the Buddha observed? What if we take his example and commit to sitting still to see what he saw?

Through sitting meditation, we can take a perspective on the separate self, or ego, and look directly at it, seeing clearly how it functions. Identifying as "I" or "me" and investigating it, we notice that the self is a form of attention concerned with our self-concept and image. When the Buddha says the self doesn't exist, he doesn't mean that this living, breathing, thinking being doesn't exist. He means that what we think of as a self doesn't correspond to reality. The idea we have of ourselves is a mental construct, one that requires maintaining and protecting. We spend a tremendous proportion of our waking hours thinking about ourselves, our hopes and dreams, and our disappointments and frustrations. These thoughts lead to actions and behaviors in the world based on a set of conclusions about our separateness. The actions we take often include managing others and controlling the environment to be safe, secure, or successful. It is a full-time job.

The perspective of the small self has a fundamental sense of its mortality and vulnerability. From this point of view, the world is a vast and unsafe place, so it makes sense that this self works to protect and maintain its identity—a completely natural function of egocentrism. This is what I learned when my heart began to malfunction. I learned that, while my life was endangered, there was another part of me that did not feel threatened and was calm in the face of that threat.

I could see my separate self more vividly because of this contrast. I could see how my ego looked out at the world from a sense of separate existence, instinctively experiencing the pressure to survive, keep it together, and strive to succeed in a highly competitive environment. It required enormous energy and focus, and it was always a moving target. That is, until my life was genuinely threatened. Then it became simple. Prior to that, attending to all of my life's details—managing thoughts, emotions, and behaviors, maintaining relationships, regulating interactions, and participating in culture, including having a job and going to school—was a stressful challenge.

But this self-project is familiar to all of us. We often want to become even better versions of ourselves. We attempt to improve, become more skilled, make more money, or achieve more status. It seems that there is no end to it. Even if we are not striving to gain wealth or status, we may be working hard to be more thoughtful, more compassionate, or better human beings. As a small self, there is no end to this experience of pressure to secure and improve.

Perhaps the most significant pain for the small self is loneliness. I felt tremendously alone when my heart malfunctioned. None of my friends could experience it with me. They cared, but they were busy, and there wasn't much they could do to actually help me. Because of the innate separateness of ego, it is always a profoundly private affair. One can never share the depth of our experience sufficiently or feel seen, heard, or supported entirely. The separation means that no one else, from a profoundly existential perspective, will ever be able to comprehend what it means to be me or you. In this separateness, we are forever alone.

Because of my health crisis, I came to see that the Buddha's insight is correct. But we can discover this through meditation by carefully observing the identity of the separate self. Of course, there are healthy expressions of self-identity. But self-identity will, by its nature, be a limited, stressful, and struggling perspective because it is separate, incomplete, and partial. Like everything in the known universe, we both are a part and whole—a holon, to use Arthur Koestler's term.[3] So, we may appear separate from the rest of reality from one point of view, but a much greater truth is that we are always part of the larger whole. The question is: How is this expansive awareness or true identity realized?

Beyond Self

Studying the Buddha's teachings means studying oneself like I did under the totem pole. As we delve deeper into the experience of sitting, we gradually begin to release the grip of self-identity. This process leads us to a profound realization that we are not alone or separate. Rather, we are intimately interconnected with everything around us. The following are several of the most famous lines from the Japanese Zen master Dogen Zenji:

> To study the Buddha way is to study the self. To study the self is to forget the self. To forget the self is to be actualized by myriad things.[4]

This is a shift in perception from being confined by the ego to embracing boundless openness, awareness, and equanimity. This experience is unmistakable and transformative. It moves us from a narrow focus on our personal identity to a broader awareness of life and existence itself. We become free from self-clinging, ideology, chronic critiques, and relentless opinions about how things should be. We encounter reality directly, freshly, and with an open mind. The Buddhist meaning of the word *emptiness* describes this open awareness without the filters of identity, the demands of agendas, or fixed interpretations of reality, simply reflecting what arises in the moment.

The absence of the past and future, dropping craving and desire, worry and concern, and the stress and aversion of self-identification is forgetting the self. To be actualized by the myriad things is to be completely connected to and informed by the world. On the park bench by the totem pole, my entire attention was captured by my distress. In the beginning, I was barely aware of the surrounding environment, including the towering evergreens, the winding sidewalks and grass, the sky, moon, and stars overhead. But as I sat quietly becoming aware and still, the grip of self-identity loosened, and the surroundings came vividly into view. I saw the light from the moon everywhere. I heard the muffled sounds at night and the silence. I felt my body and my being, and even my irregular heartbeat affirmed the fact that I was alive. My wishes that my heart rhythm would return to normal faded away as quickly as they arose. In the quiet of the night of the totem pole, the utter uniqueness of the moment was apparent; without a past or future moment to compare it to, it was precious.

From the perspective of open awareness, the ego is not bad or sinful; it is not like an agitating pest to be chased away, caught, or killed; it is simply the persistent identification with the separate self will never realize the peace and fulfillment of Buddha Nature. This natural, pristine, unconditioned awareness is our birthright and our true identity. It has been analogized to a jewel that has been sewn into our coat pocket without our knowledge. We go around for years and years looking for value, not realizing that all the time, we are endowed with an abundance of wealth.

The truth of our innate sufficiency raises questions: Why would we need to spend enormous time studying and practicing to discover what is already here? Why do we need to "study in detail," as Master Dogen says, to see our well-being is intact and not dependent on anything? We do so because our habit of self-concern separates us from this much larger identity. Practice is necessary to overcome the deeply ingrained habits of mind that divide us from reality. For Master Dogen, Zen practice itself is enlightenment.

Unique Expression

Relinquishing our attachment to the ego doesn't mean that we lose our personality, our unique gifts, or our specific talents. Self-orientation makes way for the expression of uniqueness. I was still very much myself after realizing equanimity under the totem pole.

But I was far less self-concerned and more in awe and filled with gratitude for being alive.

Zen poetry and calligraphy abound with depictions of this uniqueness—of red flowers and green willows, of straight pines and bent brambles.

Zen teacher and author of *The Snow Leopard*, Peter Matthiessen, describes,

Butter tea and wind pictures, the Crystal Mountain, and blue sheep dancing on the snow—it's quite enough.[5]

It is wonderful; it is enough. It is obvious that the painful effort of the separate self is, at some level, unnecessary. It is like slinging an extra, awkward piece of luggage over our shoulder when both hands are already full. When the clinging and anxiety of the ego are put down, and attention is open and relaxed, we are free to notice and participate in the specificity of this moment and the details of our lives.

From the point of view of practice, then, it is possible to shift to a third perspective, one we can call "unique expression." This shift is not to reify self-identity but simply to employ a skillful means that allows us to access an intimate experience of ourselves as the unique part that functions freely and easily as part of the larger whole.

When we identify as unique expression, the first recognition is that we are an utterly unique manifestation of the greater whole— nowhere else in the entire universe is there anything like us, there never has been and never will be. We are each so specific, so detailed, and so wondrous. Our interior lives are completely our own: our thoughts, feelings, and dreams. They may pass fleetingly but are particular in so doing.

Our bodies are made of specific qualities like skin tone, eye color, body shape, and gender. We inherit our DNA, which combines into an utterly unique pattern and expression. These physical traits are not permanent, yet they are the distinct, material qualities that make us up as we go. We each have families, cultural contexts, and histories with great commonalities and shared reference points, but they are entirely specific to each one of us. Awakening doesn't mean these disappear. We become more free to express them.

The occasion of our birth is our own birth, and the time and place of our death are ours, and everything in between is the detail of our distinct path—distinct and, at the same time, not separate. Further, we have an entirely unique perspective. I have heard Ken Wilber say that "enlightenment takes on a unique perspective through each of us." In the entire cosmos, we are the only ones looking through a particular lens and seeing what we see. Each of us is the only one capable of offering this perspective. Our viewpoint has an innate dignity; it is rare and intrinsically valuable. This recognition brings a kind of awe with it, a respect for ourselves and this precious human birth.

Through sitting still, we experience true interconnectedness. By letting go of attachment to separation, we can express ourselves in a way that exemplifies the harmony of the whole. Sometimes, in the Zen tradition, it is said that zazen polishes us like wood to bring out the fine grain and beauty. By experiencing our wholeness, we are free to experience our uniqueness.

And because we experience our wholeness, we are not lonely. Loneliness is not the outcome, amazement is. The answer to the loneliness problem doesn't come from a small self-identity finding the perfect relationship; it actually comes from identifying with our limitless nature and offering love and kindness in a suffering world.

The full expression of our particularity comes in the form of compassion, ethical conduct, and love for the world. Love comes in as many different forms as there are people to express it. An endless display of talents, gifts, and creativity falls from our practice as naturally as ripe fruit falls from a tree. With sufficient commitment and discipline, our unique qualities combine as unique gifts. The fulfillment of the spiritual path is in the expression of these gifts in the world. Instead of being motivated by lack, we are now moved by fullness. Instead of striving to be of service, we show up—ready and available, offering our perspective, our heart, and our skills. We no longer compete but find our true place in the world of Buddhas and Bodhisattvas, doing what we do well and naturally for others.

In the Mahayana Buddhist tradition, the Bodhisattva is one who is committed to the enlightenment, liberation, and service of all beings. Bodhisattvas make a vow not to dwell in detachment and cling to nirvana but to hang in with the persistent challenges of the human experience: in bodily form, in relationships, and in the worldly call for fairness and social justice. We vow to participate until all beings are liberated, which is another way of saying that love, ethics, and compassion become the activity of our lives. The Buddha began his spiritual search in order to alleviate human suffering. He culminated his search with this simple understanding of the role of love and of kindness.

So with a boundless heart
Should one cherish all living beings:
Radiating kindness over the entire world.[6]
—Buddha

10

THE STUDENT-TEACHER RELATIONSHIP

Diane Musho Hamilton

The prajna wisdom of enlightenment is something everyone already possesses. But you need to find a truly good friend to show you how to see your nature. —Zen Master Huineng

It's not easy to be a spiritual teacher these days. Seekers come to dharma centers looking for different things, but they are generally cautious about the person who is the teacher. Everyone is aware of the long history of abuse by people in positions of power, and American Buddhism has had its fair share of scandals related to money, sex, and other ethical breaches.

The caution is valid, but cynicism is unfortunate. It doesn't consider that every day, there are many reliable, ethical, and well-trained teachers going about the business of sharing the dharma. They host sitting groups, study the teachings with their students, and enact rituals like baby blessings, weddings, and funerals. They run organizations, manage properties, maintain websites, meet with their boards, and raise money for the benefit of their communities.

These committed Buddhist practitioners don't get paid much, but they do get up early and often, turning on lights and opening doors for people to come to meditate. They share the teachings and listen intently to the questions and suffering of others. They comfort troubled hearts and when they can, offer spiritual guidance. Most importantly, they see and feel their students' enlightened nature and help them experience it for themselves.

Teachers provide these services while dealing with criticisms, complaints, and the ever-present challenge to the legitimacy of their role. These challenges have the potential to be positive, helping the teacher mature, to clarify their ethical obligations, and to become more skilled in their use of power and authority. This maturation process is one that all leaders should hope to go through, for everyone's sake, whether they are in a teaching role or not. It seems like the maturing of our collective relationship to power is naturally occurring in human culture right now, and we should all be glad for that. (For a discussion of power in relationships, please see our book *Compassionate Conversations*, chapter 11.)[1]

Not everyone wants or needs a spiritual teacher. Some contemporary meditation adepts say that the traditional role of the teacher is archaic, while they assert that the instruction itself is priceless. But I'm not sure you can separate them so easily. It is usually the case that if we want to develop expertise or mastery in a specific area of our life, we will need the guidance of a mentor, a coach, or a teacher unless we are a born genius. We will almost certainly need a community of other committed practitioners because skills don't develop in a vacuum. Imagine an NBA player like Michael Jordan who was never coached by Phil Jackson or challenged by Larry Bird. He would never have become the stellar basketball player he was at the height of his career.

It is important to remember that Zen is training in zazen, study, ritual practice, and relationship skills with the teacher and sangha. Most fundamentally, it is a practice of paying attention to how we pay attention. So, the teacher's job is to create an environment that supports sustaining our attention on the things that matter most.

Relationship Skills

The Zen literature doesn't address relationships. Maybe because they imply the duality of self and other, or the cultural context defines them differently, or they distract from the Great Matter of Life and Death. But the student-teacher relationship *is* a relationship, and in our time and place, most of us want to develop better skills.

In the context of practice, we develop powerful human bonds and the challenges that come with them. Our bonds become strong because of the sheer amount of time we spend together and the trust that our sustained practice engenders in one another. As students, we must surrender our idealizations, own our projections, and free ourselves to show up fresh, forgiving our disappointments or hurts. But these practices cut both ways, and teachers must all do the same things.

In the context of practice, we learn to appreciate the intimacy of our humanness—our brilliant, funny moments, our confused attempts to know one another better, and the profound tenderness of our human hearts. Occasionally, we may still get mad or disgusted with each other, and sometimes we sulk or act out like little kids.

But we can unlearn some of these poorly adapted patterns, especially when the pattern is experienced in the field of open awareness and challenged in the company of good friends. Not everyone is up for this level of engagement with others, but if you seek a community with depth, the practice offers it. And as Huineng says, "We need a truly good friend to see our true nature."

Zen practice gives us a context and a method that promotes vacating negative habits of mind and seeing the reality of who we each are, directly, immediately, and without the distortions of our concepts, desires, aversions, and limiting beliefs. In other words, we practice experiencing one another clearly and simply and learn to "be for each other" in the most straightforward way.

Students have a lot to learn about practicing with their minds and emotions in relationships, and as I said, so do teachers. I am subject to similar challenges to my ego, and I trust my students to give me feedback when I am out of line. (My only ground rule is that they can't offer me feedback about my habits when I try to address one of theirs.)

Because we practice communicating, I thought asking some of my senior Zen students about their choice of engaging the practice and a teacher would be interesting. Some of them have been practicing with me for up to fifteen years, and we have weathered some of the storms of long-term relationships, but our awareness of the boundless, blue sky has always been there.

Most of the students I asked answered in Buddhist terms:

"Having a teacher has taught me how to sit upright, to harmonize breath and body, to open to the vast space of mind, and to allow my heart to feel fully."

"I have been shown the truth of impermanence so that it is a distinct feature of my experience, and I can appreciate how precious this moment is."

"I can see what emptiness means: how all things are without a fixed nature and, therefore, change. At the same time, I see how everything is interconnected, mutually influencing, and inextricably linked. This includes my life. I have the experience now that I am never separate from all that is."

One student emphasized the importance of finding a teacher who could point out ever-present awareness. "I'm not awakened," he said, "At least, I don't think my insight is very deep. Practicing with someone who consistently points me to the fundamental, ever-present, and timeless Mind has allowed me to identify with a dimension I didn't know existed. In some mysterious way, I have become kinder, even to myself."

Zen training involves dropping the preoccupation with our own perspectives, self-orientation, and preferences. One student remarked, "I have no other relationship where I am asked to surrender my preferences as the student-teacher relationship does. The actual practice, including zazen, study, and ritual, has taught me to lift my head and look around, to get beyond myself and my ingrained habits. Sometimes it involves a struggle and can be difficult, but I have learned to confront certain habits in myself. It is hard to imagine that I would have looked at some of my deeper patterns had it not been for the relationship with my teacher. The container of Zen practice itself doesn't allow me to habitually seek comfort or recoil from a challenge."

On the other hand, someone also said this: "I find a tremendous relief in the practice. I navigate my life, making decisions about many things and strategizing who I am in this context or that one. But in Zen training, I show up differently. I give up thinking about what is next; rather, I intend to be fully here, relaxing into the forms and stability of the practice, training my attention to what is. Right here and now. I can rely on the entire Zen lineage, and it is such a relief to drop my egoic concerns and attend to the whole. Truly, it is a relief."

These are powerful testimonials for a practice that reminds us that nothing can be gained from it. Instead, we practice recognizing what is already the case and expressing this recognition in our daily lives. Because of our commitment, our pain becomes manageable and our aspirations naturally include others. Generosity spills over freely and spontaneously, and the sensation is more freedom. We become more at home in our humanness, and more willing to share and serve.

Mitigating Risk, Ensuring Stability

There is always risk involved with anything in life that is worthwhile. There is so much opportunity for disappointment, disillusionment, or failure. Still, the opportunity to grow together and awaken is rare and profound, which is why the lineage persists through the generations. But one of the tasks of our time is to acknowledge how an unskilled teacher can create harm. And it is the teacher's responsibility to prevent it.

For example, the inherent intimacy of the relationship creates risk. Boundaries soften, and the natural tendency to become emotionally close or sexually involved arises. The teacher needs to understand the vulnerability on the part of the student who is looking for spiritual guidance and to draw clear boundaries so that spiritual intimacy remains distinct from personal or sexual intimacy. It isn't that there is no personal intimacy, but the wants, needs, and wounding of the personality can be redirected to the therapeutic or domestic context.

Most organizations now prohibit the sexual involvement of dharma teachers with their students in the same way that it is prohibited in therapeutic settings. This is due to the ambiguity created by dual relationships, and by the power imbalance between the teacher's authority and the student's openness, which can compromise or confuse consent. We are all aware of the increased possibility of broken hearts when erotic energy is at play or the deceit that ensues with illicit relationships. The admonition against the sexual involvement of the teacher with students also prevents the teacher from acting out lasciviously with younger, more receptive, or inexperienced students.

It helps when a student also takes responsibility, clarifying their own motives for the relationship and ruling out the idea of finding a lover in the teacher. One of my students explained how this was a factor in choosing to work with me. She said, "I feel relieved that my teacher is a woman, a straight woman at that, and that the possibility of sexual engagement is not even a thing."

Within the Zen context, the teacher is obliged to transmit the dharma directly and teach in the style of the particular school. The teacher is not there to transmit their own personal insight or leverage their charisma in a cult of personality. A lineage tradition protects students against the tendency of freestanding schools of awakening to become cults.

In our sangha, we often discuss the difference between a culture and a cult and wonder aloud what implicit pressures there may be in the sangha to conform in a way that compromises the integrity or autonomy of the student. I ask my students to surface these pressures, to talk about them, and to examine their own choices and commitments to practice, making those choices conscious.

There is a developmental process in the student-teacher relationship that begins with surrendering to the perceptions and guidance of the teacher. But like all healthy adult development, there will come a phase of differentiation. Some students will leave the practice when this happens, and they should. Some leave feeling incomplete or unsatisfied with their teacher. Others are never able to find a true home in the community. Some leave when they feel finished with their training, having received what they came for, and are ready to move on. Others receive what they didn't know they came for. For example, when I posed this question to a woman who left the practice after ten years, she said, "I learned how to be a woman from you." She didn't seem to need the dharma, the sitting, or the study, but through the practice, she found a way of expressing herself differently.

But for long-term, committed practitioners, inevitable periods of differentiation are followed by deeper integration and commitment. In this phase of practice, the student is both one with the teacher and teachings and completely unique in their expression of dharma in their own life. One student expressed the coming together and going apart of lay practice in this way:

In my circles, everyone thinks they need a self-styled spirituality. For them, spirituality is all about individuality, freedom, and constant choice. But I recognized that I could only take myself so far at a certain point. During a sesshin, I heard Roshi say, "Why not open yourself to someone else's point of view? As lay practitioners, you follow your own perceptions all day, every day. But while you are training, why not allow yourself to orient your attention to your teacher, at least while you are here?"

And that made sense. I realized I have many opportunities to go solo, embodying the training in my life and my work. I've begun to acknowledge that I have trained for over ten years, and it is up to me to manifest it. I notice two changes. First, I can relax my ego when I am working, and at the same time,

I feel more confident in myself. Not in myself exclusively but in the whole situation. And I come back to the formal practice deeply humbled. I return revitalized, with a beginner's mind as Suzuki Roshi describes. I have more questions, more curiosity, and more energy for practice.

In My Own Case

I am aware that I am humanizing the student-teacher relationship, and my description doesn't have the magical allure of depictions of the old enlightened masters and their deeply devoted disciples. In my training, I am still moved by the depth of my teacher's realization and his amazing ability to work with others. And I have memories of occasions of real magic in the form of meaningful synchronicities and powerful moments.

Once, when we were at the Shambhala Center and had walked to the stupa to pay our respects to the Vidyadhara Chögyam Trungpa Rinpoche, we stopped and turned around to look at the stupa one last time before walking down the mountain. At that moment, the full moon appeared on top of the stupa, resting right over the symbolic moon. From there, moonlight poured from the top of the stupa in all directions. It was like a crown jewel emphasizing the truth of dharma for us. I think even those who are not enchanted by magic would have been moved by this moment of beauty.

Genpo Roshi's unshakable gift was his ability to sit zazen. When he was in the zendo, sitting was a different experience. It was powerful, sustained, and vastly empty. Through him, one experienced Mind's timeless, unconditioned, and boundless nature. With his modeling, one could experience zazen as a completely natural and easeful activity. My heart was often filled with immense appreciation for the chance to practice with him and experience genuine spiritual power.

He could also be tough as a teacher, and when my ego was gripped, he would insist I let go. He challenged me to examine my unconscious will to power and invited me to own power in a more wakeful and, therefore, beneficial fashion. He pointed out that I could sometimes be emotionally needy, which was embarrassing but true. He warned me that charisma is charming but no substitute for truth. And so, he trained me to teach and lead, all the while affirming that I was a woman and at times, encouraging me to express more of my femininity.

He also had flaws and repeated mistakes in his intimate relationships. I don't know any teacher personally who doesn't have human challenges: bouts of anxiety, self-doubt, neurotic habits, moments of obvious self-centeredness, and ethical lapses. Mistakes are part and parcel of the practice, just as they are in our lives, and so are the karmic consequences. Each of us is subject to all of it. Dogen Zenji says, "When we fall to the earth, we get up from the earth." We need to be accountable for our errors. Wholeheartedness is a life that includes everything—the ups and downs, the successes and failures, and the endless stream of mistakes and recoveries.

Our practice is not to become perfect but fully and wholeheartedly human, conscious, and kind. I have been deeply humbled by the role of the student and in the role of the teacher. I know I am not a great enlightened master; I'm just a working stiff in the dharma. But I feel it is a tremendous privilege to work with my students, and they enrich my life in countless ways. One of the responses to the question I posed to my students about their choice of a teacher and practice was this:

I asked myself, "Can I live a real life in a relationship with this person?" I found the answer was yes because I realized she is a real spiritual teacher. She doesn't knock me over with special powers to get my attention. She has a different set of tools, and from my perspective, the tools are much more ordinary and helpful. I would rather learn to be present and listen than be hit with a jolt of shakti. So, my commitment flowed from that. It was just very simple. I was able to commit but for exactly the opposite reason. I didn't want only to have a spiritual experience. I wanted to live a real life.

11

RITUAL AND CEREMONY

Gabriel Kaigen Wilson

Form is emptiness, emptiness is form. —The Heart Sutra

In a recent sesshin, Roshi spontaneously led a conversation about the difference between ritual and ceremony. The discussion arose because each day in sesshin, we perform the morning service. Like all rituals, it involves a sequence of gestures, speech, and choreographed movements, as well as the use of ritual objects like candles, gongs, and incense, to convey meaning and give form to our shared intentions.

We begin by chanting the Heart Sutra, the most revered scripture in Mahayana Buddhism, and then we recite a long poem called the "Identity of Relative and Absolute." We pay homage to Kanzeon, the Bodhisattva of Compassion, and we honor our teachers and the ancestors of the lineage by reciting their names. We conclude by praying for those who are sick or who have died, and we affirm our commitment to accomplish the Buddha Way together.

Not everyone likes the role of ritual in our practice; some people are burned out from their involvement in religious rituals of their upbringing where the forms never change and the meaning seems to have vanished. Other people are made nervous by collective bowing and chanting. But many people grow to love beginning the day with an energizing, coherent, and aesthetically moving ritual structure.

In this particular sesshin, we were also engaged in a week of ceremonies to mark the rite of passage of four fellow practitioners to the status of teachers. This is called the Shiho or Dharma Transmission Ceremony. This ceremony consists of a series of rituals and smaller ceremonies in which a teacher acknowledges a student's understanding of Zen, authorizing them to teach and carry on the tradition.

A ceremony is a formal event usually involving a more elaborate set of rituals. It includes the community as participants and as witnesses and marks a momentous occasion or rite of passage. The word *ceremony* originates from the Latin *caerimonia*, which means "holiness, sacredness, awe; a reverent rite, or sacred ceremony."[1] At its best, a ceremony uses ritual forms to uplift and transform us for a moment or for the rest of our lives. They are often special events such as weddings, graduations, funerals, send-offs, or welcome homes. They can be as beautiful as they are meaningful.

Rituals and ceremonies have personal, cultural, or religious significance. They can be performed to support an intention, to bring people together to celebrate, or to recognize the accomplishment of a goal. Have you ever engaged in an activity that quiets your mind, opens your five senses, draws on the fullness of your heart, and brings your whole being into the present moment? Any act that can accomplish that is said to be life-giving.[2] The simple gesture of laying a flower on a casket, reciting vows as you look into a lover's eyes, or putting on graduation robes to walk across the stage enhances the moment, heightens our experience, and gives us inspiration, life force, and energy.

Peter Matthiessen, an American writer, environmentalist, and Zen teacher, described the transformative power of chanting homage to Kanzeon, Bodhisattva of Compassion, after learning that his wife had terminal cancer. He describes the conclusion of the chanting in this way:

But on this morning, in the near darkness—the altar candle was the only light in the long room—this immense hush had swelled and swelled, and kept on swelling as if this "I" were opening out into infinity, in eternal amplification of my Buddha being. There was no hallucination, only "I" had vanished and also "I" was everywhere. Then I let my breath go, gave myself up to immersion in all things, to a joyous belonging so overwhelming that tears of relief poured from my eyes. For the first time since unremembered childhood, I was not alone, there was no separate "I."[3]

Something Bigger

To my surprise, I have come to appreciate the transformative power of ritual and the beauty of ceremony through Zen practice. Like Peter Matthiessen, I especially value how it connects our personal experience to a much larger, shared one. Some years into my practice, I was motivated to do a solo retreat. I asked Musho Roshi's permission, and she said, "Of course, just be sure to set up an altar, and every time you open a sitting period, light the candle, offer incense, and bow to the ancestors." I did not expect Roshi to emphasize ritual in this way, but without thinking too much about it, I responded positively, saying, "Yes, of course."

Our retreat center is in Southern Utah, just a few miles outside Capitol Reef National Park. It is in the canyonlands where the vast expanse of blue sky meets an equally immense red rock landscape. The ruggedness and raw beauty of the environment constantly bring one's attention to a complete standstill as one attempts to take it all in.

The zendo, where meditation is held, is also captivating. It has an open floor plan with windows to the north and south. The layout of the sitting cushions is orderly and precise, the altar adorns and focuses the space, and a high ceiling with beautiful wood trusses expands upward.

The entire scene, both inside and outside, invites our mind and body into stillness, space, and silence.

I was invigorated the first few days of the retreat by the novelty of simply sitting by myself. The introvert inside of me loved it, and I felt strengthened by the autonomy and discipline of practicing alone. As the days went on, mind chatter quieted down, and the demand that my thoughts usually place on my attention relaxed. Soon, my experience reflected the space and stillness of the surrounding landscape and zendo. The back and knee pains that had been very prominent in my attention earlier were diminishing in relation to the openness of awareness itself.

Over a few more days, however, I started to feel lonely. My perception of the landscape I had previously enjoyed took a sharp turn, and I became aware of the harshness of the desert. The sun seemed too hot, the air was exceedingly dry, and the ancient geologic rock provoked a sensation of how insignificant I was and how short-lived my life would be compared to the millions of years of the earth around me. No matter how much I meditated, my loneliness just intensified. Halfway through one meditation period, I realized I had forgotten to light the candle, offer incense, and make my bows as Roshi had instructed. So, I stood up to perform the opening ritual, and as I did, I had a passing thought.

"How many countless practitioners throughout time have lit a candle, offered incense, and made bows to the ancestors?"

With that spontaneous inquiry, the ritual act took on a new life. My movements expanded to include the movements of all those practitioners who came before me and the ones who would come after me. As I offered incense, they offered incense. As I made bows to them, they made bows to me. As I took my seat on the meditation cushion, they took to theirs. My loneliness and separation suddenly dissolved as each ritual movement elicited new energy and excitement for this discovery. For the entire rest of the retreat, I sat alone. However, now I felt completely at home in the company of all the ancestors of the past and future.

The Problem of Routine

Ritual involves repetition, and that repetition can create a problem. Unless one can stay connected to the freshness of each moment, a ritual performed over and over can become rote, and those performing it begin to run on autopilot. I notice that when I lose connection to the life of the ritual, my mind easily strays, becoming lost in ruminations about the past or the imaginings of the future. When divided like this, ritual acts become performative and empty.

At one point, my relationship with the morning service lapsed into routine. My role at the time was to ring the bells and sound the gongs, which would initiate and accentuate many different movements within the ceremony, like bowing, chanting, and offering incense. When I first started learning the bells, I loved the experience of feeling connected to the larger whole of the service, enjoying the call and response between the bells and the other sounds and movements in the ritual.

Then, as I became more proficient with the bells, I could daydream and still deliver the appropriate sounds and timing from the bells and gongs. Or at least I thought I could. One day, someone's friend passed away while we were in retreat. Roshi invited the student to offer incense to honor their late friend during the morning ritual. Awareness that this offering was an acknowledgment of someone who had died, someone who was loved and would be missed, completely changed my experience. I brought more presence and care to sounding the gongs that day than ever before, and I could feel the difference. There was beauty, tenderness, and power in the ritual that day, and the vivid awareness of life and death pulled me out of the routine, eliciting my undivided attention. I often flash upon this memory to invoke my full attention during the service.

There is another challenge with ritual forms that we are particularly prone to in the Zen school. The precision of the Japanese rituals can become a way of judging ourselves and others harshly. We put an inordinate amount of importance on doing them properly. Then, we criticize others for doing them wrong, even wielding power inappropriately because of our experience and expertise. This lording over others is a tendency to which everyone is susceptible. It is peculiar, given how much we hate it when people lord it over us.

I can laugh about it now, but during my first Zen retreat, I experienced an interaction with a senior practitioner who reeked of what we call the "stink of Zen." I was learning how to take my seat on the meditation cushion properly. There is a series of three bows. The first occurs when you enter the zendo, and the second happens right in front of your cushion. Then, you turn around and make the third bow to the person directly across from you before you sit down.

As I turned to make the third bow, the senior monk said in a terse, even aggressive manner, "*Never* turn your back to the altar!" Yikes! Apparently, I had turned away from the altar rather than toward it! I felt embarrassed and sufficiently shamed, but I also noticed a spike in hostility in my system. I am amazed by how much communication passes between people in the zendo, though most of it is unspoken.

Later, we had a chance to talk about what happened between us. In unpacking the experience, the senior monk revealed that he felt competitive with me, perhaps even vulnerable. He was older than me by thirty years, and he was one of the more seasoned monks in the practice, someone to whom Roshi turned for support and leadership. In short, he had status.

By contrast, I was only twenty-five years old and had never been on a meditation retreat, let alone a Zen sesshin. But Roshi had given me more attention than usual because of her commitment to training a younger generation of practitioners, and I had displayed my enthusiasm for Zen practice to her. The senior monk did not like sharing the teacher's attention with a new student who, from his perspective, hadn't earned it. He said he also felt vulnerable because of the age difference, which made him feel obsolete in his role. So, he did what any proud practitioner would do—he put me in my place.

As we talked, I started to see that I had a role in this dynamic.

Somewhat unconsciously, I had been communicating defiance to him. He was in a leadership role in the zendo, and I had subtly ignored his prompts and rebelled quietly against his authority. I didn't show him my enthusiasm for practice; instead, I was half-hearted, casual, and even sloppy when I knew he was watching me. Acknowledging this was difficult, but I was involved in this power struggle.

But the conversation completely changed our dynamic, and it was the beginning of a true friendship. After we both apologized, I changed my behavior in the zendo. My bows became sincere, and when I turned to bow to the person across the way, they were infused with respect. I noticed the elegance of his hands in the prayer position and the calm in his face. I thought to myself, "If that is what practicing Zen makes you look like, I'm in."

I appreciate what Zen teacher Zenju Earthlyn Manuel says about Zen rituals: "Every student must contend with the question, do you feel controlled by the rituals, or are they leading you in silence to the place of compassion and insight?"[4]

Zazen as Ritual

I sometimes imagine an early human ancestor enjoying a prehistoric walkabout, looking for food or scoping out a resting spot. In my mind, I see them taking a moment to scan the sunlit landscape and then taking their seat in the shade on an open plain. Their movements are completely natural and relaxed. They are at home in their own skin with an innate understanding that "I am" and that this "I am-ness" is utterly consistent with everything in the natural world.

I've connected this image to how Zen Master Dogen describes zazen. It is seen "not as a means to attaining some result but as a ritual enactment and expression of awakened awareness."[5] He asserts that we do not meditate to acquire True Nature or to become a Buddha. We meditate because we already are that. In the same way, the early ancestor in my imagination did not meditate to realize "I am-ness." His simply sitting down is an expression of this innate truth.

I had a vivid experience once when my perception shifted from the usual acquiring mind, the one who sits to accomplish or gain something, to meditation being an enactment of enlightened awareness. It was the evening meditation period; the light from outside was dim as the sun was setting, and the zendo was filled with the silhouettes of bodies in silent, seated meditation postures. I could identify the outline of people by their shapes but could not make out their faces.

I was in the early phase of my practice and still becoming accustomed to sitting cross-legged. By this time of night, I was coping with fatigue, soreness, and pain in my back and legs. My thoughts careened from the pain to why I was sitting, suffering like this.

Musho Roshi was not in the zendo because she was holding one-on-one interviews with students who had questions about their practice. Halfway through the last sitting period, Roshi returned to the zendo. Instead of going straight to her seat, she lingered by the door. After a few moments, she punctuated the silence by saying, "Consider, Who is sitting right now?"

For whatever reason, this served as a turning phrase for me. Instead of attempting to answer the question, I spontaneously took a deep breath, lengthening the exhale. The stillness was potent, and the silence expressed itself completely. Nothing else could be added to the moment. Then I raised my gaze to see the outline of other meditators, and again, the question, "Who is sitting right now?" filled the room. The whole of everyone sitting together in the evening light was the only response.

For the rest of that sitting period, I no longer coped with pain, wished my experience were different, or imagined a moment in the future when I would become enlightened. The ritual act of meditation revealed the aliveness of this moment, its totality, and its embodiment in us. Zen Master Dogen says, "When even for a moment you sit upright in samadhi expressing the Buddha mudra (form) in the three activities [body, speech, and thought], the whole world of phenomena becomes the Buddha mudra and the entire sky turns into enlightenment."[6]

Zen practice has taught me to appreciate the power of ritual, employing it to uplift myself, others, and most importantly, this moment. But you do not need to be in a Zen monastery to practice rituals and ceremonies. Countless moments may be acknowledged and heightened through even the most modest ritual forms. Perhaps a friend has lost a loved one, so you light a candle, speak the deceased person's name, and enter silence for a minute or two. Maybe you have completed a project you poured your heart into, so you want to thank all the influences that supported it coming into being. So, you make a simple bow and, as Maezumi Roshi says at the end of many of his dharma talks, "Appreciate your life."[7]

12

OUR DEEPEST QUESTIONS

Diane Musho Hamilton

What is this? —Zen Question

I love questions that three- or four-year-olds ask. You know the kind. Questions such as, "Why does that dog's belly have spots?" or "Why do carrots grow in the ground?" or "How did the stars get up there?" They ask a stream of questions about everyday marvels. Their questions are simple, innocent, and genuine, even though some aren't easy to answer.

Psychologists tell us that at this age, children are eager to learn about the world around them, and they are rapidly developing language, conversational turn-taking, and cognitive skills. Children as young as two may pose a litany of "why" questions, but they are not asking for reasoning or an explanation like a ten-year-old might. They experience the words' power and ability to elicit a response. That is not to say they aren't learning from our answers, but their developmental task is multifaceted, which is why one question leads to another and then to another.

Children ask plenty of "why" questions, but they also ask "what," "how," "who," or "when." Their questions may relate to objects, people, and circumstances in their immediate surroundings, as well as their bodies, emotions, and, often, what they can and can't do. At a young age, they may question abstract concepts such as time, cause and effect, and even God.

Because their questions seem endless, taking them seriously is difficult. Offering one explanation after another in an endless stream of "why" questions is exhausting—that is, if you believe that providing a reasonable answer is the point. Instead, the inevitable fatigue may clue us in to what is important in their questioning—the sheer display of their curiosity, their capacity to pay attention to everything, and their natural ability to learn. Maybe the answers are less important than we think. Perhaps we need to learn how to respond rather than try to answer them.

I remember a scene from the Dutch movie *Antonia's Line* where Antonia and her three-year-old grandchild ride through a small Dutch village on the back of a huge draft horse as the child asks her questions.

As the horse clops along through the village, the little three-year-old asks her grandmother, who is sitting behind her on the horse, "Why is the world made up of nothing?"

And her grandmother responds, "That is why there is so much of it."

Kinds of Questions

Questions that are important to us vary, and what is a significant question depends almost entirely on the person, context, and purpose. Once, at a dinner party with a highly successful friend, I teased that I had just gone to a meeting where the organization's leader had spoken nonstop for four hours about his vision for the future. I told my friend I left the meeting exhausted, and then, as an afterthought, I asked him what he would have done had he been in my shoes.

He responded flatly, "How much is he paying you?"

That question never even crossed my mind.

Of course, if you are in business, that question comes to mind right away, but it didn't occur to me. Business people ask different questions than coaches. Coaches ask different questions than lawyers.

Lawyers ask different questions than mediators. Coaches are often encouraged to ask only open-ended questions of their clients, questions that invite the clients to ponder, consider, and explore. Lawyers use open-ended questions with their witnesses to elicit relevant information and support their case. They ask leading questions of witnesses for the other side to challenge their credibility and create doubt in judges and juries about their testimony.

As a mediator, I ask open-ended questions that encourage exploration, such as "What would you like to accomplish today? Or "What values are most at stake when you consider this conflict?"

But I also ask narrowing questions, such as "What options can you think of that would solve this?" Or "Of those three options, which is most satisfying?"

And I ask closed-ended questions that allow only a yes or no response: "Are you truly satisfied with this agreement?"

These questions function to move clients closer to an agreement. They have very different purposes and create different outcomes than those asked by a coach, a lawyer in a trial, or a consultant in a business setting. They are also different from the questions asked by Maezumi Roshi.

When I was young, I was encouraged to ask the question, "What do I want to do with my life?" I have heard many people say that question was useful to them in finding their path forward at different stages of their lives. But that question always failed me. When I would ask it, I would come up with everything or nothing and usually just end up confused or demoralized.

At one point, when I was approaching thirty and feeling the pressure to decide how best to make my living, I finally gave up on "What do I want?" Instead, I asked, "What are people telling me I am good at?" Within a month, I had several incidents of significant feedback. People said that I seemed to have a knack for helping people in conflict find a way to resolve it. And then I saw a job advertised at the local Dispute Resolution Center, and my work in conflict resolution began. It was such a fruitful reframe that I am glad I changed questions.

Questions allow us to reframe reality, think differently, and create a pause for deeper receptivity and reflection. Zen practice is the perfect place to bring questions that elude easy answers, analysis, or rational understanding. There are many of these in our lives, such as "Who am I?" "Why am I here?" "What is true?" "Who can I trust?" or "How do I live with this heartbreak?" I have never found anything like the Zen school that helps us to inhabit a question in such a profound way.

Zen Questions

In Zen practice, questions play an essential role in meditation and self-inquiry. Our tradition emphasizes keeping questions alive, pondering everything like a child would, especially our beliefs and assumptions. In the process, we learn to relax the conceptual mind, looking directly at experience and allowing ourselves to respond naturally, as Antonia does to her granddaughter.

One day, I was listening to a talk by Taizan Maezumi Roshi, a Japanese Zen master who founded the Zen Center of Los Angeles in 1967. He began his talk with the question "What is it?" And then he went on:

"What is this?"

"What is this life?"

"Dogen Zenji says: 'This is the life of Shakyamuni Buddha.'"

"What does that mean?"

"This very Mind is the Buddha."

"What does that mean?

"What is this Mind?"

"What is this Buddha business?" (My favorite).

"What is the difference between my body and mind, and that very body and mind which is Shakyamuni Buddha?"

"And how come this body is said to be the same as the Buddhas of the past, present, and future?"

"What is this life?"

"What is this?"

"What is THIS?"

That is more questions than a kid would ask! Maybe Roshi is rhetorically posing these questions, but these are significant questions in Zen. Perhaps he is encouraging our curiosity, our capacity to pay attention, and our natural ability to inquire and respond. He may be modeling for us how to investigate truly, how to inhabit a question and discover something new rather than look for an answer.

"What is this life?"

Dogen Zenji says, "This life is the very life of Shakyamuni Buddha." But as Maezumi Roshi asks, "What does that mean?" How can my life be the life of the Buddha?

The Chinese Master Huangpo said, "All the Buddhas and all sentient beings are nothing but the One Mind, besides which nothing exists. The One Mind alone is the Buddha."

But Maezumi Roshi isn't satisfied with that. He asks, "What does that mean?"

He questions further, "What is Mind?" and "What is Buddha?"

He knows these questions cannot be answered with our cognitive mind, but they must be sustained and lived until we come to see for ourselves.

"What is this?" begins and ends his inquiry. This is one of the most common questions posed in Zen training, and it takes us straight to the heart of the matter. When Roshi asks, particularly with his vigorous voice and potent, energetic presence, he cuts through the tired impulse to give a conceptual answer. Instead, his question brings our attention squarely to this moment, opening our eyes to everything around us. Suddenly, we are in the question right along with him and available to the sheer wonder of being alive now.

"What is this?"

Koan Study

The popular notion of koans is that they are paradoxical anecdotes or perplexing statements used in Zen training to stop the analytic mind in its tracks. But our school has more than seven hundred different koans, which are quite diverse. Many koans are taken from teaching stories passed down through the lineage; others come from sections of the sutras. They often involve dialogues between students and teachers to clarify or deepen the student's understanding. Other times, they occur between two or more masters to challenge and test each other, often ending in bursts of laughter or cheeky insults. They illuminate many different dimensions of the life of dharma study and, most importantly, help to see the myriad perspectives and an array of creative responses. Koans are filled with all kinds of questions.

It is true that koans can appear paradoxical or nonsensical and cannot be solved using the cognitive or analytic mind. As Zen Master Hakuun Yasutani says, "A koan is not an explanation or illustration of a thought or idea. If you regard a koan in this way, you miss the point." He says that koans "deal with the essence of the Dharma," and we enter into the koan, contemplating it and exploring it. With time, we can express it, and "show that all beings are Buddha."[1]

In our practice, students elect to participate in koan study as part of their training. The student is instructed on approaching the koan, contemplating its images, such as "What color is the wind?" or "Where does the candlelight go after its extinction?" Or they consider the specific scenario as it unfolds. For example:

Once a monk made a request of Joshu. "I have just entered the monastery," he said. "Please, give me instructions, Master."

Joshu asked, "Have you had your breakfast?"

"Yes, I have," replied the monk.

"Then, wash your bowls."

Students pay special attention to the dialogue, particularly the questions. What question does the master ask? Why does he ask the monk whether he has had breakfast? What is breakfast in this koan? And what does he mean by "wash your bowls"? After spending time with the koan, the student then presents their understanding to the teacher, who offers feedback or guidance. The student embodies their answer through actions or improvisation. Very rarely does a presentation involve words.

I like to think of koans like any compelling story. When we first encounter the story, it is not about us. It happened at another time and another place. But as we enter into the scenario's fine details, it becomes more familiar and more intimate. The more we come to know it, the more we begin to identify with different parts of it. Suddenly, the story seems to be all about us. We see the koan in our own lives and can now express it with our whole body and mind.

Once, I explored a koan about Ananda, the Buddha's cousin and closet disciple, in which he poses a question to Mahakashyapa. Mahakashyapa is the disciple who assumed the monastic order's leadership and became Ananda's teacher after the Buddha died.

Ananda asked Mahakashyapa, "Aside from passing on the brocade robe, was there any dharma the Buddha transmitted to you?"

Mahakashyapa called, "Ananda!"

"Yes," replied Ananda.

Mahakashyapa said, "Take down the flagpole at the temple gate!"

With these words, Ananda attained a great realization.

When I presented this koan, my teacher approved, and I went home. It was early morning, but I couldn't get a question out of my mind. I kept asking,

"Was there something more to that koan than I was seeing?"

"Was my koan presentation accurate?"

"Did Roshi know more than he was saying about the meaning of the koan?"

I was overcome with this pesky sensation that there was something more to it. So, I did something unusual. I called Genpo Roshi on his cell phone, and I said,

"Roshi, I'm sorry for bothering you, but I'm wondering about the koan I presented this morning about the exchange between Ananda and Mahakashyapa. Was there more to it?"

Roshi didn't answer my question in the same way that Mahakashyapa didn't answer Ananda's question. He just started to laugh. He immediately saw that I had become exactly like Ananda who, in the koan, wondered whether there was something more than a robe—something subtle, extra, or special—that Mahakashyapa received from the Buddha.

I was suddenly awake to the full-bodied experience of thinking there is something more and better and different, and how I compulsively search for that thing. Then I experienced a powerful release and felt again like Ananda who "suddenly attained a great realization."

Recently, I asked a monk in our practice to give a dharma talk. He loves listening to Maezumi Roshi's talks, so he posed several of the questions Maezumi Roshi asked at the beginning of the talk I described earlier. He asked, "What is this?" and "How can my life be the life of the Buddha?" His talk was very genuine and quite touching.

At the end of his talk, he asked for questions from the students listening. Several people asked him questions about his talk, his path, and how he developed his love of practice. Just before he closed, he turned to me and asked if I had a question. I asked him, "How is your life the life of the Buddha?"

He started to speak, but then he stopped himself. Instead, he looked at me sincerely, put his hands in the gratitude position, and bowed deeply.

13

BELOVED COMMUNITY

Gabriel Kaigen Wilson

Strong bonds are not made with ropes and no one can untie them. —Lao Tzu

Ananda and the Buddha were staying with the Sakyan clan, the Buddha's community of origin. Taking in the effervescent and delightful quality of the people, Ananda said, "Lord, this is half of the holy life, having admirable people as friends, companions, and colleagues." The Buddha looked at him with a gentle smile and said, "Oh, Ananda, having admirable people as friends, companions, and colleagues is actually the whole of the holy life."[1]

The Buddha was correct that humans flourish in the context of loving relationships. In his book *Triumphs of Experience*, George Vaillant, a Harvard researcher known for his work in human development, reveals findings from the most extensive study ever conducted on human happiness.[2] One of its conclusions is that "warm, intimate relationships are the most important contributing factor in the establishment of a good life." The study found that the participants who flourished in life and lived longest had reliable bonds based in intimacy, connection, and altruism.

Emotionally deep and intimate relationships, where generosity and reciprocity thrive, are invaluable. These qualities contrast sharply, however, with the traits young adults prefer to give their energy and attention to. In 2015, a survey of millennials asked them to list their most important life goals. Eighty percent responded by saying "to get rich," while another 50 percent said their main goal was "to become famous."[3] During a discussion at the Zen Center about dissatisfaction in life, Musho Roshi heard from a young man who said, "I don't understand why I am not living in Los Angeles in a club surrounded by beautiful women, doing shots with Jay-Z." Even though he laughed, he was serious.

There is an epidemic of loneliness in the United States. "Twenty-two percent of all adults in the U.S. say they often or always feel lonely or socially isolated."[4] Another study says that "one in three American adults over the age of forty-five are lonely."[5] This research shows that individuals with strong social bonds are 50 percent less likely to die prematurely than people with weak relationships. The negative impact on our health that results from a lack of connection is equal to the risk of smoking fifteen cigarettes per day and is more significant than the risks associated with obesity, excess alcohol consumption, and lack of exercise.[6]

As humans, we long for intimacy, companionship, friendship, and a community of people who share our purpose, values, and interests. This may be why the sangha, the community of practitioners that study, learn, and realize together in the Buddhist tradition, is considered one of the Three Treasures of the Buddhadharma. As the Buddha said to Ananda, "Having admirable people as friends, companions, and colleagues is actually the whole of the holy life."[7]

Healing Power of Sangha

Simply taking your place in a community's rich and nourishing energy can be healing. A very intimate, personal dimension of friendship is available in the group, and it combines with a stable, impersonal awareness rooted in zazen. The container of practice also creates a context for surrendering negative habitual patterns in relationships. A healthy community of people committed to mindfulness and basic kindness reveals the emotional patterns that create suffering.

A senior practitioner recalled the support of friendship and the unwavering strength of the sangha's presence that assisted her in releasing a traumatic experience. She remembered sitting in the zendo on a very hot day. During the meditation period, she spontaneously took deep breaths, leading to a positive and expansive state. Then, suddenly, that expansiveness contracted into a profound state of panic. She recounted the urgency of her thoughts:

"I need to get out of this room!"
"I need to find Roshi!"
"I need my husband now!"

Despite the urgency and panic, her training gave her the resolve to keep sitting. Eventually, the intensity passed, and the panic dissipated. However, several hours later, when she returned to the zendo for a dharma talk, she felt the contraction and panic rising again. Coincidentally, as Musho Roshi began her talk, she said to the group, "Before we begin today, I want to ask how everyone is doing."

The senior practitioner raised her hand and spoke.

"I'm having a hard time," she said, describing the panic she had experienced earlier in the day.

Her distress created a wave of unease in the group, so Roshi invited everyone to quiet their minds and become present to their fellow practitioner. Then Roshi asked for permission: "Are you willing to have the group's attention with you now?"

The student nodded.

Then Roshi said softly, "We are just going to be here with you in this. I think you might be releasing trauma from the intensity of your baby's birth four months ago."

This suggestion rang true for the student. She placed her head on her knees, and she began to cry. She cried and cried for about ten minutes while Roshi encouraged her to stay in her body, to breathe, to relax fully, and to befriend all of her experience. One student moved closer to give her energetic support, placing one gentle hand on her shoulder without interfering with her process. The rest of the group did what they knew to do together. They sat still and remained very present.

When her emotional release was complete, she lifted her head from her knees and looked around at everyone's faces, receiving love and support from the group, free of the need to comfort or console her. She was highly coherent, having experienced embodied release and integration of her traumatic memory. She was available to the presence of the sangha, which was open, boundless, and aware without any conditions or expectations of her.

Fritz Perls, the German psychiatrist and founder of Gestalt therapy, says, "Awareness is curative."[8] In reflecting on this experience, the senior student says, "Because of our practice, I experienced deep friendship infused with a vast, impersonal, and palpable energy that allowed my process to unfold. I was held without anxiety or stress, and freed of expectations of what should or shouldn't happen. Altogether, it was love."

She recalled that while she had suffered a series of panic attacks in the four months since giving birth, after the emotional release in the sangha, she has not had any anxious episodes. She attributes this to the shared commitment to mindfulness, the sustained practice of zazen, and the trust in the open hearts of her fellow practitioners. Zen practice is a boundless field in which relationships may flourish.

Dissolving Old Patterns

Families of origin are difficult places to grow up. We experience both positive and negative dimensions of relationships. We are subject to belief systems, value sets, and emotional responses to life. Some are productive; others are seriously damaging to our psyches. Roshi tells the story of a friend whose mother had schizophrenia. The friend remembers walking into the kitchen when she was five or six years old, where her mother was loudly scolding the cupboards. The friend thought to herself, "This isn't going to be good for me."

We adapt to all manner of difficult conditions: unresolved emotional pain, mental illness, abuse, and worldly stress. Some of these adaptations, whether withdrawal, overwork, anger and criticality, sexual misconduct, or habitual conflict, are problematic to the health of our future relationships. Sangha provides a practice container where frequent interruptions to our early relational patterning create opportunities to grow and change, freeing us from unnecessary suffering. (In our practice, Roshi refers practitioners to mental health and trauma-informed therapists when students need specific psychological support.)

Another senior student recalls a sea change that occurred in relation to himself. He describes coming to "the shocking realization that making a mistake in the sangha did not result in verbal, emotional, or physical abuse." These were consequences routinely doled out by his father whenever he erred.

But when he made a mistake during sesshin—sounding the gong at the wrong time, tracking mud into the zendo, or becoming angry in his communications—he had the relieving experience of being met with respect and forgiveness while still being held accountable. The sangha consistently responded to him in ways he did not expect, creating a new meaning in his mind where mistakes are not flaws in his character but one of the many flavors of practice. His body was learning to relax in the light of positive regard instead of contracting in an atmosphere of threat, anxiety, and shame.

This acceptance unlocked a new, powerful self-acceptance in him. As is commonly the case, he had blamed himself for his father's abuse, convinced that he must have deserved it. However, through the sangha's response to his errors, he is learning to stop blaming himself and just to experience and correct them. He said, "My work isn't done. I no longer blame myself but have shifted the blame to my dad."

There was one more movement to his healing journey. This student had learned to suppress his anger in an effort not to be like his father. But like his father, when he did express it, it was aggressive. Through our sangha practice, he had opportunities to hear how his angry outbursts affected other people. He heard that he became energetically intense, self-righteous, and hurtful. Most importantly, the angry outbursts undermined his friendships. We have a ground rule in the sangha: "Be For Each Other." But when he expressed his anger, he lost the connection to that ground rule, and his friends felt he was against them.

In receiving this feedback, he was not shamed nor made wrong. But he was challenged to consciously express the truth in his angry responses but to dial it down and use it in support of relationships. He came to the realization that instead of bottling his anger, he could befriend it, temper it, and take the blame out of it. This led him to befriend his father. He said, "Being in the presence of people who love you through mistakes is incredibly healing."

He was at home with himself in a way he had never experienced before. He was motivated to visit his elderly dad who was losing cognitive capacity and no longer lucid. On the occasion of his visit, however, his father was able to be fully present with him. Our dharma brother experienced this reunion as a profound blessing because he connected with his father from this new, open place, which was immensely gratifying. As life would have it, his father passed away shortly after their visit together.

Be Yourself, the World Will Give You Feedback

During Zen retreats, there is a group work period called samu. During this period, food is prepared; grounds are raked, weeded, and beautified; bathrooms are refreshed; and the zendo is cleaned and reset for the next sitting period. As a senior student says, "If you really want to get to know someone, work in the kitchen together." Samu provides countless opportunities to navigate different temperaments, viewpoints, communication styles, and emotional states. Working with others brings our intentions to life, and we have to respond in the moment to our differences. We are challenged to make clear requests and agreements, navigate miscommunications, and work with disappointment when something doesn't meet our expectations.

The best analogy I have heard is that growing in sangha is like being a stone in a rock tumbler. We start out with many rough edges, but over years of being tumbled, our rough edges give way to smooth, rounded surfaces. I have experienced this in my practice.

Out of all of my fellow practitioners, there is one person that I tangle with at every retreat. In the early years, our conflicts would take a long time to work through. Once, he accused me of power tripping in my new role as zendo leader.

He said, "You should watch your tone. Your telling people to pick up their pace during the walking meditation sounded demanding."

"A tone?" I said incredulously.

"Yeah!" he said, ironically, in a demanding tone.

"What are you talking about, dude? People were moving a little slowly, and I said, "Let's pick up the pace."

"Be honest. You meant that I was moving slowly!"

He wasn't wrong. He was moving slowly, causing a traffic jam in the walking meditation line. (Busted!)

I said, "Relax, man. I'm unsure what is happening, but you are taking it too personally."

This conversation was tense and completely lacking in skills. We blamed one another instead of speaking from our first-person experience. We ignored our emotions as though they were irrelevant. We gave negative feedback without making any requests. We failed to identify a shared value or goal, and we didn't problem-solve. We made no eye contact for the remainder of the day, nor did we speak. It was painful. But sometimes, it is necessary to experience stuckness to be willing to employ the practices that help the wheels keep turning.

In this case, we talked it over later that night. He discovered he was irritable because his back was hurting, and I realized I could have spoken to him privately rather than admonishing the whole room to speed up. It was easy to resolve when we both had time to think it over and soften our attitudes.

Mindful, honest, and authentic communication helps to free up our negative patterns. We learn to identify our egoic attachments and relax the fixation on our exclusive perspective. We don't need to completely relinquish our own truths, but we must be willing to notice our fixed positions and, instead, cultivate curiosity for another perspective. We imagine that two truths are better than one, allowing space for both viewpoints to have a place. This allows us to move quickly through the cycle of feedback, listening and learning, and moving forward with new agreements. Maturity in the sangha is captured in how short our learning cycles are. For an entire community to learn like this is a joyful game changer.

Buddha as Sangha

Thich Nhat Hanh, the Vietnamese Zen master, is known to have famously said that the "next Buddha is the Sangha." The idea that the community will hold spiritual authority and guidance is popular now. It is captured in the life and work of the late Congressman John Lewis. He was a civil rights leader and student of Martin Luther King Jr. They preached civil disobedience rooted in nonviolence to challenge the racial segregation and oppression of their time. Beloved community—that is, "a nation and world society at peace with itself"—was the vision Dr. King and Lewis actively worked toward. [9]

Throughout John's life, he was arrested over forty times for his nonviolent protesting. He led a march across the Edmund Pettus Bridge from Selma to Montgomery on March 7, 1965, to demand voting rights for African Americans. It was known as Bloody Sunday because the protesters encountered an extremely violent police response involving tear gas, billy clubs, dogs, and horse-mounted officers. John's skull was cracked open from two blows to the head. And yet, not one of the protestors acted violently in response. Bloody

Sunday shocked the nation and galvanized support for the civil rights movement. Two days later, John Lewis was back on the front lines, pursuing nonviolent social action.

People often asked him, "How could you be arrested and beaten and never strike back? How did you remain nonviolent?" His response was always clear and straight to the point: "Because I knew the beloved community was already done." He said, "Live like you are already there, that you are already in that community, that one family and one house. If you visualize it, if you can have faith it is there, for you, it is already there."[10]

John's statement, "It is already done," rests on the wisdom that sees the labels of Black and White as illusory constructs and that sees police officers not as the enemy but as the divine in human form. Living from this truth meant that John would not hit you because he loved you, and even in a struggle, he treated you like his own brother or sister.

From this holistic vision, beloved community is the True Nature of things. But as we are taught in Zen training, Buddha Nature is abundant in each person, but it is not realized without practice.[11] John practiced sincerely and rigorously with his community of nonviolent protestors. They practiced role-playing. He says,

> We went through the motions of someone harassing you, calling you out of your name, pulling you out of your seat, pulling your chair from under you, someone kicking you, or pretending to spit on you. Sometimes we did pour cold water on someone, never hot—but we went through the motions. This was drama because we wanted it to feel like we were in the actual situation where this could happen. So when the time came, we were ready. We were prepared.

The training created deep bonds, which John Lewis describes as the embodiment of beloved community.

In the same way, Zen training creates an experience of unity among those who sit together. Within our practice, we share an intention, enact our purpose, and cultivate care for one another. We find intimacy, companionship, friendship, and a community of people who gather together in the same way that people have for over a thousand years. It seems old-fashioned to say it, but we know who will be at our weddings and who will come to our funerals. We celebrate together when a new baby is born or offer support when a member experiences misfortune or loss. We maintain a connection to the lineage of ancestors from the past and prepare for an uncertain future together. We experience beloved community as already done.

14

ETHICAL TRAINING

Diane Musho Hamilton

Happiness is an activity of the soul expressing complete virtue.

—Aristotle

In Zen, training in ethics is extremely important, but it can be challenging to teach. I am not entirely sure why, but I sometimes see students' eyes glaze over and energy drain out of their bodies when I open the subject. When I ask why, they report associating the word *ethics* with old-school religious rules, demands for blind obedience, or tedious moralizing.

Ethics form the basis of a coherent and principled society, but I sometimes struggle to help students make a direct, energetic connection to their own lives. It is almost as though ethical conduct is a given, and to study its importance is to point out the obvious. My challenge as a teacher, then, is to explore conscience, moral reasoning, and ethical decision-making as a creative and life-giving process, not a set of fixed rules pertaining to right and wrong.

And yet, the simple definition of ethics is agreed-upon guidelines or rules that form the basis for conduct within a culture, sector, or school. They vary from culture to culture and even from developmental level to developmental level. What is considered ethical conduct within the Mafia or drug cartels is far from sound in a court of law. Medical ethics share elements with legal ethics but differ in that in the medical context, ethics emphasize well-being while legal ethics apply to the administration of justice. There are even differences related to gender identity when it comes to values of care or justice.[1]

The study of ethics is as necessary to character development as practicing scales is to becoming a musician. Like any art form, the more we study and practice, the more the basics matter. And as we learn, we encounter more nuances, complexities, and challenges that expand our unique moral capacity. Ethical decisions form the basis of our actions, and our actions give rise to confidence in our choice-making. Sometimes, it is difficult to know how to act, but without deliberate action, it is impossible to mature and develop a moral center.

The deeper we go, the more the ethics art form unfolds, revealing dilemmas, dynamic paradoxes, shifting social mores, and unresolvable issues, all of which have led me to a more profound commitment to ethical conduct. I have discovered that the study and practice of ethics doesn't drain life force. Instead, it contributes to greater engagement, wholeness, and aliveness because it reveals our interconnectedness with all of life. In Zen training, ethics is part of cultivating mindfulness, where paying attention to our motives, thoughts, emotional responses, and actions support greater awareness of our choices, and of their consequences and impact on ourselves and others over time.

The Zen Precepts

In Buddhist terms, ethics fall under the category of *sila*, or right conduct, one of three pillars of Buddhist practice, along with meditation (*samadhi*) and wisdom (*prajna*). Ethical behavior creates a foundation for meditation to stabilize and for wisdom to flourish. Habits of bad behavior inevitably create turmoil in oneself and conflict with others, and in that atmosphere of mental and emotional turbulence, it is impossible to sit still. To develop a stable sitting practice, a practitioner must seriously consider reducing inner turmoil and decreasing tension with others. For that, we ask to receive the precepts, and by working with them, inner calm is attained, and wisdom and compassion can be naturally expressed.

Within our Zen school, the sixteen Bodhisattva precepts are the guidelines and principles we commit to, supporting our endeavor to awaken.[2] They are based upon the Bodhisattva ideal, the aspiration to attain enlightenment for the benefit of all beings, not just oneself. The initial precepts, the Three Vows, invite us to commit ourselves to the path. The next set, called the Three Pure Precepts, simply asks us to do good, refrain from evil, and relieve the suffering of other beings. The Ten Grave Precepts, which make sixteen, resemble the Ten Commandments in that they admonish us not to kill, steal, misuse sexuality, and so forth. In contemporary practice, sometimes they are expressed positively so that not lying is framed as speaking truthfully, and not elevating oneself is described as cultivating humility.

Zen practitioners receive the Bodhisattva precepts in a formal ceremony called Jukai from a teacher or master, and from then on, these precepts become a trustable companion in accomplishing the Way. We are encouraged to explore them in our own lives, noticing which precepts are easy to enact while identifying those that are difficult to adhere to. Sometimes, we are encouraged to take a moral inventory, much like a young student of Catholicism examines their conscience at the end of the day.

In our training, the tone is different than in church. We are not shamed or reprimanded; we are encouraged to notice the benefit of the precepts when enacted successfully. We are supported in our inquiry and challenged to go further in our practice. The world of ethical conduct comes alive as we see interconnectedness more clearly and sense significant ethical nuances. Like Louis Armstrong said, "The highest level of technique is nuance." It becomes vivid and compelling to explore our ethical choices. As a part of the inquiry, we must also confront how often we fail to keep the precepts, and the practice of atonement or apology is built in to help us account for our ethical lapses.

Most importantly, the study and practice of ethics means our group creates deeper and more trusting relationships. We intentionally cultivate shared values and are willing to be accountable to each other. When conflicts arise, we have a skill set we can rely on, and people generally treat each other well. The depth of relationships positively impacts our members, and our Zen sangha functions as a refuge from the disillusionment of corruption, colliding worldviews, and moral ambiguity.

I recently witnessed a fruitful conversation regarding an ethical decision facing one sangha member. He disclosed that he had been married and had two children but had divorced four years ago. He had remained in an amicable relationship with his former wife but also developed another love relationship, which had become important to him. However, he and his ex-wife had recently become closer again because of some issues related to one of their children. It had suddenly occurred to both of them that a reconciliation might be possible.

He communicated he was open to a possible reconciliation with his former wife, but so far, he has resisted discussing this with his new companion. He felt she would break up with him if she knew about this, so he didn't want to jump the gun. He valued this relationship, and he didn't want to hurt her. As he presented his situation to the class, others listened, asked questions, and empathized. Naturally, different people identified with different perspectives, and he could see himself in their reflections.

Throughout the conversation, he became more certain about his obligation to be forthright with his girlfriend about the change in status with his ex-wife. He understood he was avoiding pain and needed to prepare for that. One group member reminded him that he didn't need to relieve the pain—hers or his own—but be present to it. Finally, he needed to prepare to sincerely listen to what she had to say. He left the class feeling confident and ready for the conversation.

Ethical Dilemmas, Moral Impossibilities

We can simply relate to these Bodhisattva precepts as a list of dos and don'ts. But our situation is far more complex—and interesting—than that. As we begin to engage with the precepts seriously, we soon see the complexity of our situation and how easy it is to fail. For example, we vow to be generous but are trying to stick to a budget. We promise to refrain from using intoxicants, but some of us seem to find psychedelics supportive of our practice. We vow not to misuse sexuality but enjoy the excitement of an erotic fantasy during a long period of sitting.

And the dos and don'ts often conflict with one another. For example, we vow to be honest, and we also promise to be kind. So, like the student in the example, we feel torn between telling the truth and sparing their feelings. We commit to not disparaging others but complain to the teacher when we disapprove of others in an effort to be open about our struggles. We promise not to speak ill of the Three Treasures, but we have to question the fact that no female teachers are in the lineage chart.

These dilemmas are ongoing. Sometimes, they result in more clarity, but they can also give rise to ethical lapses, complacency, or an unwillingness to look closely because it is uncomfortable. The contradictions can be stressful or confusing. And they can engender feelings of hopelessness. And yet, when engaged mindfully, the challenges help us deepen our consideration, coming into direct contact with our values, commitments, and choice-making. Practicing the precepts elicits a lifelong koan that will eventually transform us because our inability to succeed corresponds to how much we will change.

Under some conditions, breaking a precept is an ethical act. In one of his talks, Tenkei Coppens Roshi, who is Dutch, takes these dilemmas to another level of consideration. "Imagine it is 1943," he says. "You live in Amsterdam and have a Jewish family hiding in your home. Nazis knock on the door, asking if you are sheltering any Jews. Do you lie?"

He points out that under the circumstances, the very fact that you have chosen to secretly harbor Jews implies that you are already willing to lie, and you will continue to lie when the Nazis come to the door. And yet, lying in this situation is a courageous choice in the service of protecting the innocent. He says that sometimes we must violate one precept to uphold another and that there is a hierarchy of ethical decisions depending on the situation. Life is not static, and conditions change, and so do our ethical calculations. Talk to anyone involved in wartime strife, and you will hear how treacherous conditions create difficult, even impossible, dilemmas. The very act of trying to survive may harm others.

Many scenarios leave us with the conclusion that there wasn't an ethical solution to our dilemma. I remember how difficult it was to persuade my mother to leave her assisted living facility during the pandemic. I repeatedly invited her to stay with me in my home, out of range of the coronavirus. However, she insisted on staying in assisted living because she didn't want to burden me. Inevitably, she contracted COVID-19 before the vaccinations became available, and she died about a year later from a cardiac arrest brought on by her long COVID-19 symptoms, in her case, inflammation around her heart.

I believe this was my mother's decision, but I still wonder if I could have done more. Could I have educated her better about the risk of staying? Could I have insisted she leave or I would not pay her fees? Should I have engaged my siblings to help? I often imagine that I just didn't try hard enough. Other times, I entertain the notion that my mother had suffered enough in her old age, and perhaps it was all for the best. While others may be able to resolve these questions, I buckle under the ethical impossibility posed by the fact of her old age and death, and I don't know what to think or believe about it. So, I do my best to accept the entirety of the dilemma, allowing myself to submit to not knowing, feeling failure, and immense loss. It is painful, and it is poignant.

Living in a postcolonial, industrial, and technological society creates impossible ethical dilemmas for many of us. How can anybody who still drives a car rather than commuting by bicycle feel ethical? Is there any sound rationale for eating meat at all in the context of industrial farming? Should we still fly on jet planes, given the harsh carbon footprint? These examples merely scratch the surface of the inquiry of this scale. Like my situation with my mother, there appears to be no clear way through the ethical morass except to imagine living in a different, simpler time.

It is true that how we enact the precepts in one moment may be different in the next. It is also true that there may be circumstances with no secure ethical response. We will, no doubt, experience failure, overwhelm, and impossibility because we can't know and we can't win. But surrendering to the experience of this uncertainty changes us. We give up the idea that we can control outcomes. We become thoughtful, compassionate, and humbled by our situation. We surrender the egoic endeavor to be a "good person" and instead act with wholesome intent from moment to moment. We naturally empty ourselves of a do-gooder identity, one who constantly looks for recognition for our generous acts. And we discover, as the Sufi poet Hafiz says, "Look what happens to the scale when love holds it. It stops working."[3]

We can't solve these issues, but we can share in them and learn to love our predicament. The purpose of the precepts is not to make us saints. It is to train our minds in ethical considerations and to sensitize us to how inextricably interconnected we are. The practice brings us into greater intimacy with our lives and values, and allows us to witness the beautiful process of developing a moral center. Our intention matters. We must keep asking, "What is the most wise and compassionate response now?"

Endless Practice

How do we cultivate an understanding of ethics and deepen our character? Immanuel Kant, a German philosopher during the Enlightenment, believed that our independent ability to reason and reflect was the source of our morality. He famously said:

> Two things fill my mind with ever-increasing wonder and awe, the more often and the more intensely the reflection dwells on them: The starry heavens above me and the moral law within me.[4]

Kant's use of the word *law* is noteworthy here. He believed that our moral choices should be capable of being applied universally. They should not depend on personal preferences or circumstances. He articulated his renowned "categorical imperative" like this: "Act only according to that maxim by which you can at the same time will that it should become a universal law."[5]

But we live in the postmodern era in which we are acutely aware that our decisions are informed by subjectivity: our specific values, personal history, emotions, and hidden biases. From an integral point of view, objectivity and subjectivity have a role in our decision-making. Our remarkable capacity to look outward, to engage our rational minds, and, at the same time, to reflect on our unique circumstances makes ethical development an art form, not a set of givens. We don't need to jettison our relationship to the objective, universal, or rational, but we can and should include subjective information. Both perspectives can inform us.

We also live in a time when our evolutionary biology invites us to include our bodily intelligence. Recent research has shown that our ethical sensitivities are not born originally of rationality but arise first from our ancient sensing and feeling bodies.[6] For sound ethical thinking and action, our gut instincts, intuition, and emotions must be joined to our cognition and context so that our moral decisions become thinking, feeling, and fully embodied acts.[7]

From a Zen perspective, practicing the precepts is to encounter each moment freshly, with a beginner's mind, but with an eye toward what is fair and a heart that cares for the whole. When we listen to our moral intuition, fulfilling the precepts, examining different perspectives, and honoring the connection between ourselves and others to the best of our ability, we are soothed and inspired by the sensations of harmony and mutuality. When we disregard them, we are confronted with the pain caused by separation. Chögam Trungpa Rinpoche said something that has always been helpful to me: "Be yourself. The world will give you feedback." We can learn from our actions and develop strength of character.

At a societal level, this harmony is expressed in aspirations such as fairness and justice. The same is true when we act unharmoniously socially, generating disconnection, division, and threat, which solidifies as injustice and oppression at larger scales. But since interconnectedness is our innate condition, we can discover how what is good for you may also be good for us. We can continue to think, feel, and reflect, aligning our actions with our highest intentions. In doing so, we will, over time, foster integrity, compassion, and, as Kant said, wonder. Wise, compassionate activity is the crown jewel of Zen practice.

Original Precepts

Emily Dickinson writes, "The Truth outlasts the Sun."[8] Her words convey the recognition that the truth of our interdependence is immutable and not a human construct. She implies that truth will outlast even the most potent source of energy and life. The Buddha taught that we are not separate from all that is; instead, we are deeply embedded in mutually dependent and influencing conditions. Sometimes, this is expressed as Indra's net, a metaphor that describes a net with a jewel at each intersection, where each jewel reflects every other jewel in the net. But we must realize it for ourselves, embodying and manifesting this wholeness in our actions.

This perception has a profound impact on our way of being. When the rigid distinction between self and other dissolves, profound compassion, patience, and creativity arise. However, there is a common misconception that the enlightenment experience necessarily leads to ethical behavior. This is often not the case.

A spiritual teacher attended one of our retreats as a participant. He sincerely confronted his missteps as a teacher that led to the dissolution of his practice community. In this particular retreat, we were studying the precepts. I mentioned that sometimes, after a powerful enlightenment experience, there is a stage that can negatively impact our relationship with others precisely because we see that there is no "self" and no "other."

The spiritual teacher had insight into his situation and said to the group,

> The distinction you are making is helping me. Everything I did as a teacher, I believed, was for my students' awakening. I saw that our sense of self is fundamentally neither real nor ultimate. And because it is not real, I honestly felt that there was no one to hurt. My interventions were often harsh and punitive in service of helping my students relinquish their attachments and transcend their egos. But I see now that I caused pain and unnecessary suffering. I was so identified with oneness, I lost sight of our two-ness: our distinctness, sovereignty, and autonomy.

In the Zen tradition, we say that the realization of the absolute is not yet enlightenment. We must realize our True Nature, inseparable from others, and express it through compassionate action that alleviates suffering and awakens beings. In our school, the lifelong practice of the not-one-not-two is enlightenment.

Endless Practice

In the last chapter of his life, the historical Buddha faced significant challenges, not unlike the challenges we face now. Devadatta was a young, talented cousin of the Buddha. He was also a disciple who became ambitious and rivalrous, resentful of what he perceived as the Buddha's authority over the order of monks. He decided to build a power base and began ruthlessly promoting himself. He curried the favor of a prince who became his patron and helped him to consolidate power. Devadatta tried to divide the community and even attempted to assassinate the Buddha himself.

If that wasn't enough, there are some accounts of further tensions the Buddha endured. There is some evidence that a war resulted from a dispute related to water resources. The Buddha's people, the Sakyans, clashed with the neighboring clan over rights to the river, which flowed through their territories. The conflict escalated, and the Sakyans were eventually defeated. Many were killed in the fight.[9]

It is hard to imagine the Buddha, having committed himself to teaching the dharma, ethics, compassion, and nonviolence throughout his life, confronted by deceit, division, and war. I imagine these experiences would be utterly disheartening, inducing doubt in dharma itself. But the Buddha was unwavering. In a dharma talk after the massacre of his people, he said that realizing our True Nature and practicing the precepts would benefit a virtuous man or woman even in this world.[10] Because as Emily Dickinson said, "The Truth outlasts the Sun."

15

A LINEAGE TRADITION

Gabriel Kaigen Wilson

All of you who are reading this quote and studying these teachings are part of this lineage. —Chögyam Trungpa Rinpoche

When I asked my teacher to receive the precepts (Jukai) and committed myself to practice within the Zen Buddhist tradition, I was invited to complete a kechimyaku. The Japanese word *kechimyaku* means a vein, a blood lineage, or a genealogy and refers to an actual lineage chart made on rice paper. I was instructed to trace the lineage chart, drawing one continuous, winding line in red pencil, weaving across the page.

This red line represents the continuous flow of time, and on it, I wrote the names of successive masters back through the generations to Shakyamuni Buddha himself. For most Zen students, making this chart is the first time we carefully examine the direct line of our Buddha ancestors, and it is often the beginning of contemplating ourselves as part of a historical lineage of dedicated spiritual seekers.

Our human lives occur along that winding line, belonging to a thirteen-billion-year stretch of time that fills our minds with the images of cosmic evolution and tales of human history. The human story is filled with many kinds of lineages running from the past into the present. Our genetic code involves a series of mutations that connect us to our ancestors and place us within a genetic line. These are our familial, genealogical lines, both the matrilineal and patrilineal sides. There are anthropological, or evolutionary, lineages where our DNA can be traced back to the family of hominids, which includes the great apes such as orangutans, gorillas, chimpanzees, and bonobos.

There are artistic lineages and musical streams of influence. Lineages occur in athletics, dance, and martial arts. Scientific lineages involve the development of theories explored and built up over time, and important historical figures such as Galileo, Newton, and Einstein are masters of these scientific ideas. There are religious and spiritual lineages. As I said, a Zen lineage describes the line of succession of Buddhist teachers who passed down teachings and practices from generation to generation, beginning with Shakyamuni Buddha himself.

Zen emphasizes the importance of lineage because the realization of the true nature of Mind requires direct contact between master and disciple (or teacher and student), sometimes described as "Mind-to-Mind" or "face-to-face" transmission.[1] This intimate connection lies at the heart of Zen practice because the realization of one's True Nature goes beyond words, concepts, or even written texts; it must be experienced. Direct experience is essential in understanding and embodying Zen. The student-teacher relationship also serves to preserve the teachings' authenticity because they are passed directly from one generation to the next.

Thus, the intimacy of face-to-face transmission between teacher and student in the past, present, and future has been the lifeblood of the Buddha ancestors. The preservation of the dharma is the most essential matter for Buddhists.[2]

Like all lineages, the Zen lineage provides continuity with the past. By participating in the same study and practice as their Zen ancestors, Zen practitioners belong to a succession of spiritual seekers who dedicate themselves to the realization of enlightenment. It is also said that while engaged in the actual practice of upright sitting, or zazen, the essential mind of the practitioner is the same as the ancestors. This Mind is beyond space and time and is the same as all the past, present, and future Buddhas. This powerful connection is a tremendous source of inspiration for maintaining the tradition and passing it on to future generations.

In studying the lineage and coming to know the masters and their particular stories, we begin to see ourselves as part of it. When I studied cosmology in college, I had a similar experience. We attempted to map the universe's lineage from its big bang origins to the fullness of life on Earth as we now know it. But when I studied it, my frame of mind was divided. I imagined that I stood apart from the cosmos and its evolutionary process. In other words, "I" (Gabe) and "it" (the cosmos) were separate.

It wasn't until a health crisis confronted me with my own mortality and, paradoxically, opened my mind to the sheer wonder of being alive that I could place myself inside the universe's evolution. For the first time, I felt a direct connection between the Big Bang and my own beating heart. When I connected to the cosmological lineage in this way, I realized I belonged here.

Original Lineage

Two thousand five hundred years ago, Shakyamuni Buddha trained his student Mahakashyapa in meditation, guiding him to recognize his enlightened nature. Eventually, the Buddha gave Mahakashyapa the spiritual authority and responsibility of maintaining the practice lineage. This transmission was symbolized by giving him a robe and bowl. The robe represented the Buddha's teaching and the l'beration from suffering, while the bowl represented the monastic tradition of living simply and surviving on alms and the generosity of others.[3]

By giving Mahakashyapa dharma transmission, the Buddha recognized his student's meditative clarity and ability to carry on the Buddha's teaching after he died. Mahakashyapa's transmission is the beginning of the Buddhist lineage. The popular master Bodhidharma, famous for his heavy eyebrows and formidable gaze, brought Buddhism from India to China and is considered the first Zen ancestor. As such, the lineage has been "directly transmitted, Mind to Mind from teacher to student"[4] for hundreds of years up to the student-teacher relationship of today. (Apparently, there are some gaps in the lineage story, but the commitment to continuity is unshakable).

The completion of the kechimyaku is a part of every Jukai ceremony and symbolizes this unbroken line of transmission, as I said. After each student completes the drawing of the lineage chart, they hand over the kechimyaku to their teacher. As part of the ceremony, the kechimyaku is signed, sealed, incensed, and returned to the student.

After the Jukai ceremony, I remember receiving it back and unrolling it later that evening. I reviewed the flowing red line I had drawn and the many names of the masters over eighty-plus generations of practice since the Buddha. But something had changed. My new dharma name had been added right below my teacher's name. This had a profound impact on me. I still recognized the names of the Zen masters, but now I saw myself among them. I could feel how they walked the very path I was walking, and they became like friends who had gone through the same ups and downs, struggles, and letting go, just like I had. And for the first time, I appeared in their company.

This allowed me to connect to their stories even more intimately than before. If you were to have asked me before the ceremony, "How is your story similar to the Buddha's story?" I would have laughed because the Buddha was so exalted in my mind that to make that comparison was ludicrous. But now, having completed the kechimyaku, I could clearly see my own story in the Buddha's.

Siddhartha Gautama grew up with wealth and privilege, but he became restless with it. He conscripted one of his servants to take him beyond the palace walls and into the wide world outside. Once outside, he encountered a sick person, an old person, and a corpse.[5] It was his first encounter with suffering, inevitable change, and the unavoidable fact of mortality. It shook him to the core, just like my confrontation with my mortality, and like me, it changed him forever. The Buddha then saw the serene face of a monk, which inspired him to seek that same serenity, just like I did when I recognized the equanimity that pervaded my experience under the totem pole.

I viewed myself *as* one of the ancestors when I saw my name on the lineage chart. But I began to see myself as one *with* them when I heard the story of Huineng. His story began when he was illiterate and poor, making ends meet by selling firewood in the marketplace. One day, he heard someone recite a verse from the Diamond Sutra, and suddenly, his mind felt "clear and awake."[6]

Huineng approached the person who had repeated the words from the sutra and asked where the scripture had come from. He learned it had come from the monastery of the Fifth Chinese Patriarch, Master Hongren. Huineng immediately set out for this monastery. After a long journey, Huineng arrived and paid his respects to Master Hongren.

"Where are you from? And what do you hope to accomplish by paying your respects?" Master Hongren asked.

"I am from Lingnan, and the reason I came all this way to pay my respects is for just one thing: to become a Buddha," said Huineng.

Master Hongren scoffed, "But you are from Lingnan and a jungle dog at that. How could you possibly become a Buddha?"

Huineng replied, "People might be from the north or south, but not their Buddha Nature. The bodies of this jungle dog and the Master are not the same, but how can our Buddha Natures differ?" At the moment Master Hongren was about to reply, other students arrived, and Huineng was sent to pound rice for the practicing students, which he did for the next eight months, never entering the meditation hall.[7]

During this time, Master Hongren brought his students together, asking each of them to write him a poem expressing what they had realized through their practice. He explained that whoever expressed the clearest realization in their poem would receive dharma transmission and assume the function of the teacher. The most senior monk was favored to receive dharma transmission, given his years of practice and dedication. I naturally saw myself more like this monk in the story than Huineng because he was a hard worker, willing to strive and sustain his efforts to accomplish what he wanted. The senior monk, Shenxiu, wrote this poem:

> The body is the Tree of Wisdom,
> The mind but a bright mirror.
> At all times diligently polish it,
> To remain untainted by dust.[8]

Master Hongren read this poem, perceiving the monk's insight, but he also saw that insight was incomplete. The poem represented the mind as a mirror that had to be kept free of dust. This implied you could accomplish this through effort, expressing a gap between oneself and one's inherent Buddha Nature.

Huineng overheard the students reciting this poem, and he knew immediately what Master Hongren knew: that whoever wrote the poem had not completely realized their True Nature. Huineng, illiterate as he was, asked one of the students to write down a poem that he wanted to post in response.

> The Tree of Wisdom fundamentally does not exist.
> Nor is there a stand for the mirror.
> Originally, there is not a single thing,
> So where should dust alight?[9]

The first time I read Huineng's poem, I suddenly tasted again that equanimity, spaciousness, and remarkable stillness I recognized amid my health crisis. Unexpectedly, this moment disrupted the notion that the experience at the totem pole was mine alone. I saw it was the same experience that every person has, meditator or not, who encounters the present moment completely undivided, free of thoughts of past or future or feelings of hope or fear. This True Nature is timeless, having no beginning or end. This realization is transmitted through time, from generation to generation.

Compassionate Activity

The lineage is preserved through practice, study, ritual, and the student-teacher relationship. The most enduring element of this lineage is Mind-to-Mind transmission of the true dharma. And the desire to share with others naturally occurs. It is beautifully captured in this exchange between Diane and her teacher, Genpo Merzel Roshi.

As a student, Diane went to dokusan, a private interview with her teacher, to discuss her practice. He opened their time together with a question:

"Why are you here?"

"To practice and realize," Diane responded.

Genpo Roshi paused, considered her response, and then posed this question:

"What about others?" he asked.

That question, "What about others?," is the essential question of Mahayana Buddhism. For those who practice in the Mahayana school, to which Zen belongs, a Bodhisattva, or one who is awakened, defers the bliss of nirvana, choosing instead to remain engaged with the world and its strife until all beings have been liberated from suffering.

In this tradition, the experience of freedom is accompanied by the spirit of compassion. Therefore, one's practice naturally includes others. The expression of compassion provides vitality, energy, and joyful activity in support of others' spiritual awakening. This altruistic impulse, expressed in the Bodhisattva vow,[10] motivates us to share the dharma and support the well-being of others, ensuring the preservation of the teachings over lifetimes.

Imagine Genpo Roshi's teacher, Taizan Maezumi Roshi, who was born in Japan in 1931 and trained at Sōj-ji Zen monastery, a large training temple located outside of Tokyo since 740. His Zen training was the same as that of his father, Baian Hakujan Kuroda, and Maezumi Roshi received dharma transmission from him. (Maezumi Roshi received dharma transmission from three different teachers in three lineages of Zen.)

Maezumi Roshi came to Los Angeles at age twenty-six as a priest at Zenshuji Temple, the Soto headquarters in the United States. Upon relocating, he encountered a culture wildly different in its conventions and sensibilities from Japan. When he established the Zen Center of Los Angeles about ten years later, in 1967, many of his students were from the counterculture in California. They were throwing off the traditions of their parents and relatives, experimenting with their lives in all kinds of new ways. Some were from secular backgrounds, with little or no religious training, while others were raised in the religion of their upbringing, only to reject it to search for their own unique path. Most were college educated, with degrees in science, education, psychology, or the humanities. Some studied martial arts, others embraced free love or psychedelics, while still others were involved in the civil rights and feminist movements of the time.

Zen had a particular appeal during this period in the United States with the blooming of the consciousness movement of the sixties and seventies. But the Zen experience wasn't like the New Age workshops, encounter groups, or human potential weekends at Esalen. Maezumi Roshi taught Zen thoroughly and traditionally: sesshins were silent, still, and long; dharma talks were formal and the ritual forms precise.

The casualness of American culture was replaced with discipline and decorum, and the students learned that Zen training wasn't about improving your self-care or honing your personal preferences. In fact, Zen teachers have extolled their students for centuries to expect nothing, seek nothing, and grasp nothing. This is a hard sell in an acquisitive, self-oriented culture like ours. And in the beginning, this sentiment is just not comforting.

But in the long run, it is freeing. Maezumi Roshi had faith in the training as it was transmitted to him and believed it suitable for planting the seeds of Zen in American soil. But he also knew that for the practice to take root and flourish, some aspects of the lineage would need to evolve. Zazen, particularly shikantaza, remains the unshakable heart of the practice, as well as the ever-dependable face-to-face transmission from teacher to student. But other things are changing.

Our sangha emphasizes healthy relationships because young people want authenticity in relationships and need skills for it. Psychology often takes on a bigger role in the West, as students may be encouraged to do psychotherapeutic, embodiment, or couples' work. Certainly, Zen culture in North America has collective work to do regarding power dynamics, privilege, and hidden biases to succeed in being genuinely inclusive and socially awake. And *eco-dharma* is already a common term used for the intersection of ecology and dharma that recognizes our well-being rests on realizing interconnectedness, maintaining respect for all life, and seeking protection of the natural world.

Genpo Roshi says that Maezumi Roshi told his successors, "I have taught you all I know. Now, as Westerners, you are best suited to explore how to preserve the dharma while sharing it in ways that Western minds will understand."

Maezumi Roshi's compassionate activity—his elegant expression of authentic Japanese Zen practice marked by aesthetic precision, evocative ceremonies, and subtle meanings—sometimes stands in sharp contrast to the practical, down-to-earth style of some Zen practice in the West. But while the cultures may differ, the kindness that unlocks zendo doors for sitting, that opens dharma books to hear from the old masters, that serves endless cups of coffee and tea in support of the community, and that bends an ear to listen intently to the longing of people everywhere to live a fuller, more complete life is exactly the same. It is the same kindness, exactly.

Sincere guidance belongs neither to the cultures of the East or West, North or South, for that matter. Genuine encouragement doesn't depend on our ethnic group, and presence itself has nothing to do with our politics. Compassion is the natural activity of enlightenment and lies beyond identity altogether. It is recognized across all cultures around the world; in fact, it is recognized across time and throughout the entire human story.

Maezumi Roshi was asked by a filmmaker once if he believed in the soul. Roshi reflected quietly and then responded, "I don't know about the soul. What I know about is the vow. It carries us from moment to moment and across lifetimes." One who embodies the Bodhisattva vow is dedicated to awakening—our own and others' from moment to moment and across time. It is this vow that gives our lives continuity, purpose, and beauty, and keeps the lineage alive and well for generations to come.

16

COMMITMENT TO PRACTICE

Diane Musho Hamilton

Continuous practice creates the circle of the way.
—Dogen Zenji

Gabe and I were brought to Zen practice through specific existential challenges in our early adult lives. I lost seven friends in a few short months, and he was confronted with his own mortality because of his heart's arrhythmia. Drawn to sitting still in response to impermanence and suffering, we experienced the clarity and calm that sitting zazen affords. Gabe says that after sitting through longer retreats, he felt revitalized, coherent, and healthy. I found that just sitting for a week or longer relieved my existential anxiety. My heart opened to others, my energy flowed freely, and I felt deeply at home in the atmosphere of dharma practice and study. The practice takes us beyond our interest in self-improvement and even personal well-being, but one can't help but notice its positive impacts.

The Buddhist path invites commitment to wakeful, wholehearted engagement with each moment. Those moments add up, and it has now been over forty years since I started meditating and twelve years since Gabe and I have been practicing Zen together. We have experienced the inevitable ups and downs of our commitment—times of inspiration and vision and times of boredom and cool. Some difficult moments have come and gone, while easy moments have flowed one into another. Old habits have been worn down, while creativity bubbles spontaneously and joy rises up often.

As our practice ripens over time, the relationship to time itself changes. Often, you can feel the practice stretch back for a thousand years through the forests of India, over the plateaus of China, and far into the mountains and valleys of Japan. Somehow, it landed in North America, where it has taken root. The practice is far bigger and much older than we are, so one senses it beyond oneself and one's individual efforts. This reflection expands our perspective even more, and Dogen Zenji's insight that ours is the continuous practice of all of the Buddhas of the past, present, and future is real.

The Spiritual Marketplace

As seekers embarking on a spiritual path, we are likely to sample different methods, teachings, teachers, and communities to see what appeals to our minds and nourishes our souls. This is an exciting time of exploration, especially now that we have access to the world's great traditions through travel, education, and the internet. The choices on the spiritual menu are abundant and diverse, catering to very different sensibilities, wants, and needs. Like looking at a sumptuous menu in a new restaurant, we want to try everything. We want to sample and taste, share and compare what we like and what we don't.

We can choose from the vast growing-up menu by trying a weekend of transformational coaching to recognize the full force of choice in shaping our destiny. Or find a health and fitness website to learn all about physical well-being, from the use of supplements for health to important changes in diet or how to improve our sleep hygiene. We can engage in positive psychology for better self-esteem or attend a communications workshop to authentically engage with others or to have better sexual relations. We can explore the esoteric world of entheogens to heal our wounds and open our minds. It is a huge menu today; sometimes it is overwhelming.

The potential pitfall during the sampling phase is accumulating experiences rather than establishing a proper practice. Chöygam Trungpa Rinpoche said we can easily become spiritual materialists.[1] We fail to either wake up or grow up because we don't establish roots, investing time, care, and energy in one method. To deepen, we must commit. As Rinpoche says, "To work on ourselves is really only possible when there are no sidetracks, no exits. Working on oneself, without such exits or sidetracks, is the Buddhist path."[2]

We can opt for a waking-up approach—meditating for calm, concentration, presence, and mindfulness in all of our activities. A commitment to dharma as a prominent feature in one's life changes things. We may decide to reorganize our lives like Gabe did so that dharma is the priority. Our conduct may come into harmony with our values through studying the precepts, and with the help of a teacher, we may experience a powerful shift from self-identity to Buddha Nature, the one we share with all beings. We may commit to a Buddhist path because the practice has power and momentum beyond our personal will.

Taking Your Seat

Committing to Buddhist practice is not for everyone, but sustained commitment is essential for both waking up and growing up. We chose the Zen path, following Rinpoche's advice and sticking with the practice of just sitting. We also included our approach to growing up, improving our social skills, communicating more completely, and being for one another.

Gabe was all in for a true enlightenment experience. He recalls how single-mindedly he pursued a big opening, or kensho. He focused intensively on this goal and organized his life so that he could attend more meditation retreats. Eventually, he moved to Salt Lake City to engage in daily zazen and train with me. He often asked my permission to stay an extra week after a retreat to continue practicing zazen on his own. He reminded me of the young Alexander Hamilton in the musical, who described himself as "young, scrappy, and hungry."

In our tradition, we say that a committed practice involves great faith, great doubt, and great determination. Great faith doesn't come from belief. There is no gap between faith and direct experience. It is faith in arousing the thought of enlightenment, in practicing and realizing all beings are Buddha. It is faith in the truth of the teaching.

Once, I coached Gabe on the importance of confidence in his practice. In our private meeting, I said, "I will disappoint you because I am human. But as to your awakening, I will not disappoint. I have tremendous faith in zazen, in this lineage tradition, and its teachings. Most importantly, I trust your True Nature, and your capacity to practice and experience enlightened mind directly. My own teacher had that confidence, and he instilled it in me. I hope I can do the same for you."

He was determined to have a profound breakthrough. One day, he pressed me about it, expressing his frustration. At that moment, I was aware that as a woman teacher, I might not meet his drive in the way a male teacher might. So I said, "My teacher, Genpo Roshi, is coming to town soon. Why don't you pose your question to him?"

The evening rolled around, and when Genpo Roshi gave his talk, Gabe was ready with his question. "I am seeking a big opening. What should I do?"

He looked at Gabe, unimpressed, and answered, "You just need to realize there is nothing to get." And then he moved on to the next person whose hand was up, not checking in to see if Gabe had a follow-up comment.

Gabe was highly disappointed in Genpo Roshi's answer. He wanted to be given something of value, some direction, affirmation, or at least a drop of hope. Roshi didn't offer those. Gabe was also indignant. He laughs about it now, saying, "Didn't he know I graduated from Stanford? I deserved a better response!"

But in *Cutting Through Spiritual Materialism*, Chögyam Trungpa Rinpoche says, "Disappointment is the best chariot to use on the path of the dharma. It does not confirm the existence of our ego and its dreams."[3] The Zen tradition emphasizes the role of doubt to undermine our reliance on the conceptual mind and the motives of our limited sense of self. We must actively doubt our experience of separation, of being insufficient, or our belief that something is wrong. Eventually, the striving of the ego for answers and constant affirmation collapses, and true letting go occurs.

That opening, or awakening, allows us access to an undivided reality where we instantly belong. But we don't overcome our doubt; doubt overcomes us, and we surrender the motives of the ego. There comes a point when we can see what Genpo Roshi meant when he said there really is nothing to get or to achieve. What we seek is already here, and yet it is entirely ungraspable. You can't possess it, sell it, buy it, or commodify it in any way. It is the true source of our practice, but we won't realize it without a full commitment to practice.

So, we have to be determined. Over time, Gabe's raw ambition gave way to the routine of practice in much the same way a young athlete has to learn to play team ball after years of showing off in neighborhood pick-up games. Instead of fueling his desire for a big opening, the day-in and day-out of healthy discipline and sustained effort tempered his passion, instilling it deeper into his system and his life. He has become consistently committed to practice and is inspired by his experiences. However, I have noticed him move beyond his conventional preferences and desire for dramatic results. He just keeps doing it, rain or shine. His practice has matured and deepened, creating a throughline between formal meditation retreats, daily sitting, and everyday life. He is less concerned with a single experience because he recognizes that his practice is his whole life.

Lives of Others

When writing about continuous practice, Master Dogen said, "Your practice affects the entire earth and the entire sky in the ten directions."[4] It is such a powerful and positive vision. He also says, "Even if we doubt it, it is so." At the close of each day, we recite the Four Vows together. We commit to serving others and accomplishing the Way together. This reminds us that we live in an amazing reality of interconnectedness and reciprocity. The meaning of belonging comes to life in the context of practice and in the fullness of giving and receiving.

Sometimes, it is difficult to pinpoint the effects of practice on oneself. But it is easy to see in others. Gabe recounts his experience with his wife, Alana, during the birth of their first child. He describes that the labor had become so intense that she inquired about an epidural to relieve the pain. Moments later, they were told that the baby was coming, so an epidural couldn't be given. It was time to push. Alana immediately dropped the promise of relief and pushed with her whole body and being. He says that witnessing her full participation in bringing their daughter into this world was a moving expression of engaging body and mind wholeheartedly.

Once their daughter arrived, the doctor who attended the delivery said to Alana, "I'm so impressed by you. What did you do to prepare for this?" The doula jumped in and said, "She has practiced meditation for ten years." The doctor replied, "Oh, wow. Well, I can't really prescribe that to my patients—they only have nine months." She walked toward the door, then paused, turned back to Alana, and said, "Well, you were amazing, Mama."

The second story is about a senior student of mine, Rob, a beautiful man, athletic as a Greek god, who is unwaveringly devoted to the Zen path. He is only forty-six but recently had a serious heart attack while playing hockey at the local rink. His friends immediately called 911, the ambulance arrived in no time, and in the middle of the onslaught of emergency medicine, he managed to connect wholeheartedly with the EMTs, cracking jokes and thanking them as he was swept away in the ambulance. His true love and wife, Brooke, had rushed down from the stands and was there with him the whole time. At one point, turning to her in the midst of that emotional intensity, he asked her to text me to thank me for the practice.

Another Zen student, Tomer, who is Israeli, gave a dharma talk entitled "You Are Always Where You Are Supposed to Be." He described how, in his work with adolescent students, he encouraged them to accept that here and now is always the best place to be. He finds it a helpful reminder for his young students who are focused on their futures. It was a charming talk.

But during the question and answer period, I posed a challenging question to him. I asked, "Were the Israelis who were murdered and terrorized by Hamas last October right where they were supposed to be? And the Palestinian civilians being killed by Israel's military right now, are they exactly where they are supposed to be?"

He paused, breathed deeply, and centered himself. The inescapable reality of the violence, brutality, and trauma at home generated tremendous presence in him. He entered a very powerful internal consideration while sitting fully exposed in front of the room. We could see and feel the pain well up in his heart, and he could feel our sadness and grief. After a few moments, he said some simple, poignant words, but I don't remember them. His quality of presence and our shared recognition of human suffering were beyond words and connected us immediately to the suffering on the other side of the world.

The Circle of the Way

Dogen Zenji says, "Between aspiration, practice, enlightenment, and nirvana, there is not a moment's gap; continuous practice is the circle of the way."[5] These four aspects of practice and commitment are seamless. The aspiration to awaken is evidence of the awakened mind itself. The very thing we seek is already here. The natural impulse to respond and to help others is inherent. We genuinely want to alleviate the suffering of others, nurture our shared aspirations, encourage each other through difficult times, and ensure future generations receive the benefits of this tradition. This is the circle of the way.

One last story. It comes as quite a surprise. My son, Willie, is thirty-five now. He has Down syndrome. His father, my ex-husband, died this last fall from cancer. He was eighty-four. They were very close pals and spent almost all of their time together: painting and drawing in the studio, playing golf, and driving in the car listening to music. They laughed and joked constantly. This is a profound loss for Willie, and he is undergoing all kinds of changes.

He has never been interested in dharma, but one day after his father died, he asked me if he could go to the Zen Center with me just to get out of the house. But he came into the practice that day like he was born there. He sat still for an hour and a half. He listened to the dharma talk, responded to questions, and went for the occasional laugh.

Last week, he attended his first sesshin. I didn't expect him to participate fully, but he did. He liked coming to the community meetings, eating meals with the group, doing the dishes during the work period, and sitting for many hours in the zendo. I just let it happen. I have been completely surprised by his ability to participate. He is treated as a complete equal in this context because Buddha Nature pervades all social ranks and can't be limited to one up or one down. His comments during the dharma talks are sincere, telling, and sometimes very moving. I just have to get out of the way, the same way I do in my own practice.

We put on a short comedy where the character of Emperor Wu was substituted with Donald Trump. Donald Trump asks Bodhidharma, who is played by Willie, some classic questions.

Trump says, "I want to make Buddhism great again. I have given so much of my wealth to building temples and supporting practice. What merit will I receive?"

Bodhidharma, played by Willie with huge, fake eyebrows, a robe, and a knapsack says, "No merit *what-so-ever*," shaking his pointer finger.

"Well," says Trump incredulously. "If I am to receive no merit, can you share what is the essence of the holy teaching?"

Willie says, "Vast emptiness, nothing but hooooly." The actual line is "Vast emptiness, nothing holy," but I couldn't get Willie to drop the "but holy."

Finally exasperated, Trump demands, "Who are you?"

And Wille replies, "I got no idea." Bodhidharma apparently says something closer to "I don't know," but Willie put his own spin on it.

"How did it happen that Willie has begun to practice Zen?" I ask myself.

"I got no idea."

ACKNOWLEDGMENTS

The idea for this book came about from a conversation with Nikko Odiseos regarding the future of Buddhism. We appreciate Shambhala Publications for encouraging us to explore this theme and for the work of our editor, Beth Frankl. Julia Sati was invaluable in her moral support, nuanced proofreading, and editing skills. Many thanks to Alana Felt, Leonardo Wilson, and Michael Zimmerman for reading our chapters and providing their input and feedback. We are grateful to the Dragon Heart Sangha members for generously sharing their stories. As ever, we are deeply indebted to Ken Wilber for his work and influence on our lives and practice.

NOTES

Introduction

1. Ken Wilber, *Integral Meditation: Mindfulness as a Way to Grow up, Wake up, and Show up in Your Life* (Boulder, CO: Shambhala, 2016).
2. Ken Wilber, *The Religion of Tomorrow: A Vision for the Future of the Great Traditions—More Inclusive, More Comprehensive, More Complete* (Boulder, CO: Shambhala, 2018).

1. Zen and Growing Up

1. Ken Wilber, "The Further Reaches of Human Nature," in *Sex, Ecology, Spirituality: The Spirit of Evolution* (Boston: Shambhala, 1995), 262–86.
2. Robert Kegan, "The Growth and Loss of the Institutional Self," in *The Evolving Self* (Cambridge, MA: Harvard University Press, 1982).
3. Kegan, *The Evolving Self*, 253.
4. Ken Wilber, *Integral Spirituality: A Startling New Role for Religion in the Modern and Postmodern World* (Boston: Integral Books, 2006), 88–93.
5. H. M. Chandler, "The Transcendental Meditation Program," vol. 2 of *Consciousness-Based Education*, ed. Christopher Jones (Fairfield, IA: Maharishi International University Press, 2011).
6. Robert Kegan, *In Over Our Heads: The Mental Demands of Modern Life* (Cambridge, MA: Harvard University Press, 1994), 330.

7. Dōgen and Kazuaki Tanahashi, *Treasury of the True Dharma Eye: Zen Master Dogen's Shobo Genzo* (Boston: Shambhala, 2013), 30.

2. Embodied Skills for Relationships

1. Stephen W. Porges, "Ancient Rituals, Contemplative Practices, and Vagal Pathways," in *Coping Rituals in Fearful Times*, ed. J. Gordon-Lennox (Cham: Springer, 2022), 43–64.
2. Stephen W. Porges, *The Polyvagal Theory: Neurophysiological Foundations of Emotions, Attachment, Communication, and Self-Regulation* (New York: W. W. Norton, 2011).

3. Developing Emotional Maturity

1. Ken Wilber, *Integral Psychology: Consciousness, Spirit, Psychology, Therapy* (Boston: Shambhala, 2008), 236n1.
2. Diane Musho Hamilton, *Everything Is Workable: A Zen Approach to Conflict Resolution* (Boston: Shambhala, 2013), 183–87.
3. Hamilton, *Everything Is Workable*.
4. Tania Singer and Olga M. Klimecki, "Empathy and Compassion," *Current Biology* 24, no. 18 (2014): R875–78. https://doi.org/10.1016/j.cub.2014.06.054.

4. Shadow

1. Robert Augustus Masters, *Bringing Your Shadow out of the Dark: Breaking Free from the Hidden Forces That Drive You* (Boulder, CO: Sounds True, 2018), 13.
2. Robert Augustus Masters, *Spiritual Bypassing: When Spirituality Disconnects Us from What Really Matters* (Berkeley, CA: North Atlantic Books, 2010), 1.
3. Masters, 53–54.
4. Masters, 2.

5. Ken Wilber, *Integral Spirituality: A Startling New Role for Religion in the Modern and Postmodern World* (Boston: Integral Books, 2007), 119.
6. Wilber, 128.
7. Diane Musho Hamilton, *Everything Is Workable: A Zen Approach to Conflict Resolution* (Boston: Shambhala, 2013), 157.

5. Purpose and Presence

1. James Hillman, *The Soul's Code: Character, Calling, and Fate* (New York: Random House, 1996), 9.
2. *Online Etymology Dictionary*, s.v. "calling (*n.*)," accessed January 15, 2024, www.etymonline.com/word/calling.
3. Zenju Earthlyn Manuel, "Sweeping My Heart," Lion's Roar, December 10, 2023, www.lionsroar.com/sweeping-my-heart/.
4. Manuel, "Sweeping My Heart."

6. Inspired to Wake Up

1. Dōgen and Kazuaki Tanahashi, *Treasury of the True Dharma Eye: Zen Master Dogen's Shobo Genzo* (Boston: Shambhala, 2013), 325.
2. Dōgen and Tanahashi, 324.
3. Dōgen and Tanahashi, 324.

7. Practice Is Enlightenment

1. Surya Das, *Letting Go of the Person You Used to Be: Lessons on Change, Loss and Spiritual Transformation* (London: Bantam, 2012), 29.
2. Ken Wilber, *The Religion of Tomorrow: A Vision for the Future of the Great Traditions—More Inclusive, More Comprehensive, More Complete* (Boulder, CO: Shambhala, 2018), 202.
3. Dōgen and Kazuaki Tanahashi, *Treasury of the True Dharma Eye: Zen Master Dogen's Shobo Genzo* (Boston: Shambhala, 2013), 325.

8. Just Sitting

1. Taigen Daniel Leighton, *Zen Questions: Zazen, Dōgen, and the Spirit of Creative Inquiry* (Boston: Wisdom Publications, 2011), 25.
2. Dōgen, "Fukanzazengi: Recommending Zazen to All People," trans. Kazuaki Tanahashi, accessed January 14, 2024. www.upaya.org/uploads/pdfs/Fukanzazengi.pdf.
3. Hongzhi and Taigen Daniel Leighton, *Cultivating the Empty Field: The Silent Illumination of Zen Master Hongzhi* (Boston: Tuttle, 2000), 45.
4. Stephen Addiss, Stanley Lombardo, and Judith Roitman, eds., "Universal Recommendation for Zazen," in *Zen Sourcebook: Traditional Documents from China, Korea, and Japan* (Indianapolis, IN: Hackett, 2008), 143.

9. True Identity

1. Walpola Rahula, *What the Buddha Taught* (New York: Grove Press, 1959), 10.
2. Rahula, 27.
3. Arthur Koestler, "The Holon," in *The Ghost in the Machine* (London: Hutchinson, 1967), 45–58.
4. Dōgen and Kazuaki Tanahashi, "Actualizing the Fundamental Point: Genjō Kōan," in *Moon in a Dewdrop: Writings of Zen Master Dōgen* (San Francisco, CA: North Point Press, 1995), 69–73.
5. Peter Matthiessen, *The Snow Leopard* (New York: Penguin Books, 1978), 242.
6. "Karaniya Metta Sutta: The Buddha's Words on Loving-Kindness," translated from the Pali by the Amaravati Sangha, accessed January 14, 2024, www.accesstoinsight.org/tipitaka/kn/khp/khp.9.amar.html.

10. The Student-Teacher Relationship

1. Diane Musho Hamilton, Gabriel Menegale Wilson, and Kimberly Myosai Loh, "Clarifying Power," in *Compassionate Conversations: How to Speak and Listen from the Heart* (Boulder: Shambhala, 2020), 101–10.

11. Ritual and Ceremony

1. *Online Etymology Dictionary*, s.v. "ceremony (*n.*)" accessed January 13, 2024, www.etymonline.com/search?q=ceremony.
2. Ernest Becker, *Escape from Evil* (New York: Free Press, 1985), 6.
3. Peter Matthiessen, *Nine-Headed Dragon River: Zen Journals, 1969–1985* (Boston: Shambhala, 1986), 31.
4. Zenju Earthlyn Manuel and Arai Paula Kane Robinson, *The Shamanic Bones of Zen: Revealing the Ancestral Spirit and Mystical Heart of a Sacred Tradition* (Boulder, CO: Shambhala, 2022), 31.
5. Taigen Daniel Leighton, *Zen Questions: Zazen, Dogen, and the Spirit of Creative Inquiry* (Boston: Wisdom Publications, 2011), 35.
6. Dōgen and Kazuaki Tanahashi, *Treasury of the True Dharma Eye: Zen Master Dogen's Shobo Genzo* (Boston: Shambhala, 2013), 5.
7. Hakuyū Taizan Maezumi, *Appreciate Your Life: The Essence of Zen Practice* (Boston: Shambhala, 2002).

12. Our Deepest Questions

1. Hakuyū Taizan Maezumi and Bernie Glassman, *On Zen Practice: Body, Breath, and Mind* (Somerville, MA: Wisdom Publications, 2002), 98.

13. Beloved Community

1. "Half (of the Holy Life) Upaḍḍha Sutta (SN 45:2)," accessed January 14, 2024, www.dhammatalks.org/suttas/SN/SN45_2.html.

2. George E. Vaillant, *Triumphs of Experience: The Men of the Harvard Grant Study* (Cambridge, MA: Harvard University Press, 2015), 37–41.

3. Robert Waldinger, "What Makes a Good Life? Lessons from the Longest Study on Happiness," TED video, 12:37, November 2015, www.ted.com/talks/robert_waldinger_what_makes_a_good_life_lessons_from_the_longest_study_on_happiness/.

4. Vivek H. Murthy, *Together: The Healing Power of Human Connection in a Sometimes Lonely World* (New York: HarperCollins, 2020), 10.

5. Murthy, *Together*.

6. Murthy, 13.

7. Half (of the Holy Life) Upaḍḍha Sutta (SN 45:2).

8. Frederick S. Perls and Joe Wysong, *Gestalt Therapy Verbatim* (Highland, NY: Gestalt Journal, 1992).

9. John Lewis, *Across That Bridge: Life Lessons and a Vision for Change* (New York: Hachette Books, 2016), xi.

10. "John Lewis: Love in Action," *On Being with Krista Tippett*, updated July 23, 2020, Podcast, 50:55, https://onbeing.org/programs/john-lewis-love-in-action/.

11. Dōgen and Kazuaki Tanahashi, *Treasury of the True Dharma Eye: Zen Master Dogen's Shobo Genzo* (Boston: Shambhala, 2013), 3.

14. Ethical Training

1. Carol Gilligan, "Concepts of Self and Morality," in *In a Different Voice: Psychological Theory and Women's Development* (Cambridge, MA: Harvard University Press, 1982), 64–105.

2. Robert Aitken, *The Mind of Clover: Essays in Zen Buddhist Ethics* (New York: North Point Press, 2000), 4.

3. Daniel Ladinsky, *Love Poems from God: Twelve Sacred Voices from the East and West* (New York: Penguin Compass, 2002), 238.

4. Immanuel Kant, *The Critique of Practical Reason*, trans. Thomas Kingsmill Abbott (Mineola, NY: Dover, 2012), 170.

5. Immanuel Kant, *Practical Philosophy*, ed. Mary J. Gregor (Cambridge: Cambridge University Press, 1996), 57.

6. Robert Sapolsky, "Morality and Doing the Right Thing, Once You've Realized What It Is," in *Behave: The Biology of Humans at Our Best and Worst* (London: Penguin Books, 2018), 478–520.

7. Daniel Kahneman, *Thinking, Fast and Slow* (London: Penguin Books, 2011).

8. Emily Dickenson, *The Poems of Emily Dickenson*, ed. R. W. Franklin (Cambridge, MA: Harvard University Press, 1999), poem 1495.

9. Karen Armstrong, "The Historical Context of the Buddha's Time," *Buddha* (New York: Penguin Books, 2001).

10. Armstrong, 173.

15. A Lineage Tradition

1. Dōgen and Kazuaki Tanahashi, *Treasury of the True Dharma Eye: Zen Master Dogen's Shobo Genzo* (Boston: Shambhala, 2013), 570.

2. Dōgen and Tanahashi, 569–75.

3. Dōgen and Tanahashi, 569–75.

4. Huangpo and John Blofeld, *The Zen Teaching of Huang Po: On the Transmission of Mind* (Boston: Shambala, 1994).

5. Karen Armstrong, "The Historical Context of the Buddha's Time," in *Buddha* (New York: Penguin Books, 2001).

6. Red Pine, *Zen Roots: The First Thousand Years* (Berkeley, CA: Counterpoint, 2022), 142.

7. Red Pine, 143.

8. Janet Jiryu Abels, *Making Zen Your Own: Giving Life to Twelve Key Golden Age Ancestors* (Boston: Wisdom Publications, 2012), 25.

9. Abels, 26.

10. Shantideva, Virya Paramita, chapter 7.

16. Commitment to Practice

1. Chögyam Trungpa, "The Six Realms," in *Cutting Through Spiritual Materialism*, ed. John Baker and Marvin Casper (Boston: Shambhala, 2002), 163–76.

2. Chögyam Trungpa and Carolyn Rose Gimian, *The Collected Works of Chögyam Trungpa*, vol. 3 (Boston: Shambhala, 2003), 376.

3. Trungpa, *Cutting Through Spiritual Materialism*, 25.

4. Dōgen and Kazuaki Tanahashi, *Treasury of the True Dharma Eye: Zen Master Dogen's Shobo Genzo* (Boston: Shambhala, 2013), 332.

5. Dōgen and Tanahashi, 332.

BIBLIOGRAPHY

Abels, Janet Jiryu. *Making Zen Your Own: Giving Life to Twelve Key Golden Age Ancestors*. Boston: Wisdom Publications, 2012.

Addiss, Stephen, Stanley Lombardo, and Judith Roitman, eds. "Universal Recommendation for Zazen." In *Zen Sourcebook: Traditional Documents from China, Korea, and Japan*. Indianapolis, IN: Hackett, 2008.

Aitken, Robert. *The Mind of Clover: Essays in Zen Buddhist Ethics*. New York: North Point Press, 2000.

Armstrong, Karen. *Buddha*. New York: Penguin Books, 2001.

Becker, Ernest. *Escape from Evil*. New York: Free Press, 1985.

Chandler, H. M. "The Transcendental Meditation Program." Vol. 2 of *Consciousness-Based Education*, edited by Christopher Jones. Fairfield, IA: Maharishi International University Press, 2011.

Das, Surya. *Letting Go of the Person You Used to Be: Lessons on Change, Loss and Spiritual Transformation*. London: Bantam, 2012.

Dickinson, Emily. *The Poems of Emily Dickinson*. Edited by R. W. Franklin. Cambridge, MA: Harvard University Press, 1999.

Dōgen. "Fukanzazengi: Recommending Zazen to All People." Translated by Kazuaki Tanahashi. Accessed January 14, 2024. www.upaya.org/uploads/pdfs/Fukanzazengi.pdf.

Dōgen, and Kazuaki Tanahashi. "Actualizing the Fundamental Point: Genjō Kōan." In *Moon in a Dewdrop: Writings of Zen Master Dōgen*, 69–73. San Francisco, CA: North Point Press, 1995.

————. *Treasury of the True Dharma Eye: Zen Master Dogen's Shobo Genzo*. Boston: Shambhala, 2013.

Gilligan, Carol. *In a Different Voice: Psychological Theory and Women's Development*. Cambridge, MA: Harvard University Press, 1982.

"Half (of the Holy Life) Upaḍḍha Sutta (SN 45:2)." Accessed January 14, 2024. www.dhammatalks.org/suttas/SN/SN45_2.html.

Hamilton, Diane Musho. *Everything Is Workable: A Zen Approach to Conflict Resolution*. Boston: Shambhala, 2013.

Hamilton, Diane Musho, Gabriel Menegale Wilson, and Kimberly Myosai Loh. *Compassionate Conversations: How to Speak and Listen from the Heart*. Boulder, CO: Shambhala, 2020.

Hillman, James. *The Soul's Code: Character, Calling, and Fate*. New York: Random House, 1996.

Hongzhi, and Taigen Daniel Leighton. *Cultivating the Empty Field: The Silent Illumination of Zen Master Hongzhi*. Boston: Tuttle, 2000.

Huangpo, and John Blofeld. *The Zen Teaching of Huang Po: On the Transmission of Mind*. Boston: Shambala, 1994.

"John Lewis: Love in Action." *On Being with Krista Tippett*, updated July 23, 2020. Podcast, 50:55. https://onbeing.org/programs/john -lewis-love-in-action/.

Kahneman, Daniel. *Thinking, Fast and Slow*. London: Penguin Books, 2011.

Kant, Immanuel. *The Critique of Practical Reason*. Translated by Thomas Kingsmill Abbott. Mineola, NY: Dover, 2012.

————. *Practical Philosophy*. Edited by Mary J. Gregor. Cambridge: Cambridge University Press, 1996.

"Karaniya Metta Sutta: The Buddha's Words on Loving-Kindness." Access to Insight. Accessed January 14, 2024. /www.accesstoinsight .org/tipitaka/kn/khp/khp.9.amar.html.

Kegan, Robert. *The Evolving Self: Problem and Process in Human Development*. Cambridge, MA: Harvard University Press, 2001.

————. *In Over Our Heads: The Mental Demands of Modern Life*. Cambridge, MA: Harvard University Press, 1994.

Keizan, and Francis Dojun Cook. "Case Number One: Shakyamuni." In *The Record of Transmitting the Light: Zen Master Keizan's Denkoroku*. Somerville, MA: Wisdom Publications, 2003.

Koestler, Arthur. "The Holon." In *The Ghost in the Machine*, 45–58. London: Hutchinson, 1967.

Ladinsky, Daniel. *Love Poems from God: Twelve Sacred Voices from the East and West*. New York: Penguin Compass, 2002.

Leighton, Taigen Daniel. *Zen Questions: Zazen, Dogen, and the Spirit of Creative Inquiry*. Boston: Wisdom Publications, 2011.

Lewis, John. *Across That Bridge: Life Lessons and a Vision for Change*. New York: Hachette, 2016.

Maezumi, Hakuyū Taizan. *Appreciate Your Life: The Essence of Zen Practice*. Boston: Shambhala, 2002.

Maezumi, Hakuyū Taizan, and Bernie Glassman. *On Zen Practice: Body, Breath, and Mind*. Somerville, MA: Wisdom Publications, 2002.

Manuel, Zenju Earthlyn. "Sweeping My Heart." Lion's Roar, December 10, 2023. www.lionsroar.com/sweeping-my-heart/.

Manuel, Zenju Earthlyn, and Arai Paula Kane Robinson. *The Shamanic Bones of Zen: Revealing the Ancestral Spirit and Mystical Heart of a Sacred Tradition*. Boulder, CO: Shambhala, 2022.

Masters, Robert Augustus. *Bringing Your Shadow out of the Dark: Breaking Free from the Hidden Forces That Drive You*. Boulder, CO: Sounds True, 2018.

———. *Spiritual Bypassing: When Spirituality Disconnects Us from What Really Matters*. Berkeley, CA: North Atlantic Books, 2010.

Matthiessen, Peter. *Nine-Headed Dragon River: Zen Journals, 1969–1985*. Boston: Shambhala, 1986.

———. *The Snow Leopard*. New York: Penguin Books, 1978.

Murthy, Vivek H. *Together: The Healing Power of Human Connection in a Sometimes Lonely World*. New York: HarperCollins, 2020.

Perls, Frederick S., and Joe Wysong. *Gestalt Therapy Verbatim*. Highland, NY: Gestalt Journal, 1992.

Pine, Red. *Zen Roots: The First Thousand Years*. Berkeley, CA: Counterpoint, 2022.

Porges, Stephen W. "Ancient Rituals, Contemplative Practices, and Vagal Pathways." In *Coping Rituals in Fearful Times*, edited by J. Gordon-Lennox, 43–64. Cham: Springer, 2022.

———. *The Polyvagal Theory: Neurophysiological Foundations of Emotions, Attachment, Communication, and Self-Regulation*. New York: W. W. Norton, 2011.

Rahula, Walpola. *What the Buddha Taught*. New York: Grove Press, 1959.

Sapolsky, Robert M. *Behave: The Biology of Humans at Our Best and Worst*. London: Penguin Books, 2018.

Singer, Tania, and Olga M. Klimecki. "Empathy and Compassion." *Current Biology* 24, no. 18 (2014): R875–78. https://doi.org/10.1016/j.cub.2014.06.054.

Trungpa, Chögyam, and Carolyn Rose Gimian. *The Collected Works of Chögyam Trungpa*. Vol. 3. Boston: Shambhala, 2003.

———. *Cutting Through Spiritual Materialism*. Edited by John Baker and Marvin Casper. Boston: Shambhala, 2002.

Vaillant, George E. *Triumphs of Experience: The Men of the Harvard Grant Study*. Cambridge, MA: Harvard University Press, 2015.

Waldinger, Robert. "What Makes a Good Life? Lessons from the Longest Study on Happiness." TED video, 12:37. November 2015. www.ted.com/talks/robert_waldinger_what_makes_a_good_life_lessons_from_the_longest_study_on_happiness/.

Wilber, Ken. *Integral Meditation: Mindfulness as a Way to Grow Up, Wake Up, and Show Up in Your Life*. Boulder, CO: Shambhala, 2016.

———. *Integral Psychology: Consciousness, Spirit, Psychology, Therapy*. Boston: Shambhala, 2008.

———. *Integral Spirituality: A Startling New Role for Religion in the Modern and Postmodern World*. Boston: Integral Books, 2007.

———. *The Religion of Tomorrow: A Vision for the Future of the Great Traditions—More Inclusive, More Comprehensive, More Complete*. Boulder, CO: Shambhala, 2018.

———. *Sex, Ecology, and Spirituality: The Spirit of Evolution*. Boston: Shambhala, 2000.